Bible Promises

Outlines for Christian Living

Bible Promises

Outlines for Christian Living

Martin H. Manser

Marshall Pickering

Marshall Pickering
34–42 Cleveland Street, London W1P 5FB, U.K.

British Library Cataloguing in Publication Data

Bible promises
  1. Christian life – Devotional works
  I Manser, Martin H.
  242

ISBN: 0–551–01870–4

Phototypeset in 11/12 Linotron Baskerville by
Input Typesetting Ltd, London
Printed in Great Britain by
Courier International Ltd, Tiptree, Essex

To Terry Peasley

Acknowledgments

The author expresses his appreciation of Andrew Shanks for his comments on the manuscript and Mrs Rosalind Desmond for her painstaking typing of the manuscript and compilation of the indexes.

Contents

Introduction

Bible Promises has been designed as a handbook of practical Christian living. I have chosen a selection of the promises of the Bible and have tried to see how they work out in practice.

The aim of the book is to present information and from this to draw personal encouragement and challenge. The material is arranged in six major themes. We begin with the persons of the Trinity: God the Father, the Lord Jesus Christ, and the Holy Spirit. How does our life with God find expression? In belonging to God's church and living for him in the world: these are the next major themes. And in the final theme we look forward to the future and draw together some of the chief strands of teaching on the promises of the Bible.

Each of the major themes, *Knowing God, Trusting Jesus, Growing in the Spirit, Living in the world*, etc., is divided into eight sections. Within each of the first seven, we explore a particular topic, beginning with a key thought and a key Bible verse to set the scene. After the main study material, comes a hymn (which can be used as a response), a conclusion and a final Bible quotation, all designed to help you retain the main emphases of the teaching. The final section of each theme presents further application under the heading *Working it out*.

The book has been designed particularly for personal use. Those leading small groups will also find it a helpful resource book — as may a hard-pressed preacher wanting a quick sermon outline!

In writing the book, I have tried to be honest and realistic ... about our failures as well as our successes. And its ultimate aim is to help us become more like the people God intends us to be, as we make 'his very great and precious promises' our own (2 Peter 1:4).

Martin H. Manser
October 1988

Knowing God

1

THIS IS YOUR GOD!

Key thought We need to realize afresh the great majesty of God. As we truly trust in God, we can know him at work in our lives.

Key Bible verse ' "Here is your God!" See, the Sovereign LORD comes with power' (Isaiah 40:9–10).

The greatness of God: Isaiah 40

- The Jews are in exile in Babylon. God is about to restore them to their own land. In verses 1–11 we hear tender voices from heaven speaking to Jerusalem that her time in exile is soon to come to an end: the LORD is coming! The comfort given is nothing airy-fairy but is based on four facts:

  ☐ the problem of the people's sin has been dealt with (verse 2; see also Ephesians 1:7);

  ☐ the glorious LORD is coming (verses 3–5, 9–10);

  ☐ God's word is unchanging and eternal (verse 8);

  ☐ God looks after his people, as a shepherd looks after his sheep (verse 11; see also John 10:11).

- Verses 12–26 show God as the creator and controller of all: no one is like him.

  ☐ Just look at his majestic acts in creation (verse 12). Could we do that (verses 13–14)?

  ☐ Now look at the great countries of the world, which seem so powerful. But what are they to God (verses 15–17)?

  ☐ Next, think about the world – its vast size, its teeming millions. But what is this in comparison to God (verse 22)? And what about the world's great men: the leaders of our countries and our super-powers? See them in relation to God (verses 23–24).

  ☐ Finally, think about the stars – innumerable and light years upon light years away. What are they to this God? (verse 26)

- Verses 27–28 put paid to a cynical retort, 'So what?' Are you and I asking the question of verse 27? Do we think that this unique God (verse 25) is just too great to care about his people? The fact of the matter is seen in verse 28: he is too great to fail us. He cannot fail us, he cannot forget us. He never grows old or tired; his understanding is beyond the depths of human reason.

- Verses 29–31 show us how God's power can be experienced in our lives. We may be weary, but we can trust God (verse 31; NIV 'hope in the LORD'; see also Isaiah 25:9; 26:8) and know our weak power being exchanged for his great power (verse 31).

The question of verse 25 'rebukes *wrong thoughts about God*. "Your thoughts of God are too human," said Luther to Erasmus. This is where most of us go astray. Our thoughts of God are not great enough; we fail to reckon with the reality of His limitless wisdom and power. Because we ourselves are limited and weak, we imagine that at some points God is too, and find it hard to believe that He is not. We think of God as too much like what we are. Put this mistake right, says God; learn to acknowledge the full majesty of your incomparable God and Saviour.'

The question of verse 28 'rebukes *our slowness to believe in God's majesty*. God would shame us out of our unbelief. What is the trouble? He asks: have you been imagining that I, the Creator, have grown old and tired? Has nobody ever told you the truth about Me? The rebuke is well deserved by many of us. How slow we are to believe in God *as God*, sovereign, all-seeing and almighty! How little we make of the majesty of our LORD and Saviour Christ! The need for us is to "wait upon the LORD" in meditation of His majesty, till we find our strength renewed through the writing of these things upon our hearts' (J. I. Packer, *Knowing God*).

> My God, how wonderful Thou art,
>   Thy majesty how bright!
> How beautiful Thy mercy-seat,
>   In depths of burning light!
>
> How dread are Thine eternal years,
>   O everlasting LORD,
> By prostrate spirits day and night
>   Incessantly adored!
>
> O how I fear Thee, Living God,
>   With deepest, tenderest fears,
> And worship Thee with trembling hope,
>   And penitential tears!
>
> Yet I may love Thee, too, O LORD,
>   Almighty as Thou art,
> For Thou hast stooped to ask of me
>   The love of my poor heart.
>
> How wonderful, how beautiful,
>   The sight of Thee must be,
> Thine endless wisdom, boundless power,
>   And aweful purity!
>
>   Frederick William Faber, 1814–63

Conclusion

This first step in our discovery about God and his promises is above all else a 'stop signal' to wonder and worship.

'Those who hope in the LORD will renew their strength. They will soar on wings like eagles; they will run and not grow weary, they will walk and not be faint' (Isaiah 40:31).

GOD IS SPECIAL

Key thought As we capture again a sense of God in his holiness and glory, so our own lives become renewed and we are ready to serve God.

Key Bible verse 'Mine eyes have seen the King, the LORD Almighty' (Isaiah 6:5).

The holiness of God: Isaiah 6

- What did Isaiah's vision of God show him about God (verses 1–4)? Do we see God like this?

- What did Isaiah's vision of God show him about himself and his own needs (verse 5)? (See also Luke 5:8.) 'It is integral to Isaiah's message that his words will be those of a forgiven man, himself as guilty as those to whom he will offer life or death' (Derek Kidner).

- How does God provide for Isaiah's sin (verses 6–7)? Note that the penalty for sin was paid by a substitute being sacrificed on the altar.

- Why is the order of the events in 1–7, 8–13 important? (See also Psalm 51:13.) How does this affect our lives? Are we responding to God's commission?

- Think about the message Isaiah had to take to his own people. What are we told are the unavoidable effects of rebelling against God? (See also John 3:16–21.)

What is holiness?

- To many people the whole idea of holiness is something
  negative, associated with lots of 'don'ts' – don't go to
  the cinema, don't smoke, don't drink, etc. We've lost a
  sense of the holiness of God as being his very nature.
  The original Hebrew word for *holy* has the idea of 'being
  separate', 'set apart', perhaps even 'special', which is a
  positive word. God is special! He is different. He is
  separate from everything else: he alone is God. In this
  sense, God's holiness is related to his glory (Isaiah 6:3).

- All three Persons of the Godhead are described as holy:
  □ God is holy: his names in the Old Testament include
  'the Holy One' (Job 6:10; Habakkuk 1:12) and 'the Holy
  One of Israel' (Isaiah 5:19, 30:12).
  □ The LORD Jesus Christ is holy (Mark 1:14; Luke 1:35;
  Acts 4:27).
  □ The Spirit is known as the *Holy* Spirit (Luke 11:13;
  Acts 2:5; Ephesians 4:30).

- God's holiness does not stand in isolation. He is the Holy
  One *of Israel*; there is a challenge for the people of God
  to be like him (Leviticus 11:44–45). The New Testament
  is full of calls to live a holy life (e.g. Colossians 3:1–14;
  1 Thessalonians 4:3–7; 1 Peter 1:15–16). See also Growing like Jesus, p. 86.

- God's holiness – his utter purity and his just and perfect
  rule – stands in glaring contrast with the sinfulness of
  human beings. God cannot look on evil (Habakkuk
  1:13). His justice demands his wrath against sin. God's
  wrath is not a crude fitful human 'temper tantrum', but
  'the holy revulsion of God's being against that which is
  the contradiction of his holiness' (John Murray). It is
  only by the love of God giving his Son to die on the cross
  to bear the punishment for our sin that as believers we
  can come into the presence of the holy God (Isaiah
  53:4–6; Romans 3:25; Hebrews 10:19–23).

Holy, holy, holy, L ORD God Almighty!
  Early in the morning our song shall rise to Thee;
Holy, holy, holy! merciful and mighty,
  God in Three Persons, blessed Trinity!

Holy, holy, holy! all the saints adore Thee,
  Casting down their golden crowns around the glassy
    sea;
Cherubim and seraphim falling down before Thee,
  Who wert, and art, and evermore shalt be.

Holy, holy, holy! though the darkness hide Thee,
  Though the eye of sinful man Thy glory may not see,
Only Thou art holy, there is none beside Thee
  Perfect in power, in love, and purity.

Holy, holy, holy, L ORD God Almighty!
  All Thy works shall praise Thy Name, in earth and
    sky and sea;
Holy, holy, holy! merciful and mighty,
  God in Three Persons, blessed Trinity!

Reginald Heber, 1783–1826

Conclusion

God alone is completely pure and free from all evil.
  So it is not possible for those who do wrong to
  come into the presence of God until they have
  been made clean.

'Holy, holy, holy is the L ORD Almighty; the whole
  earth is full of his glory' (Isaiah 6:3).

THE FRIENDSHIP OF GOD

Key thought By his grace, God commits himself to people. He calls us to be his friends and to follow him in the world.

Key Bible verse 'I will ... be your God, and you will be my people' (Leviticus 26:12).

A special relationship

- 'I will be your God and you will be my people.' This sentence, with slight variations, occurs again and again throughout the Bible (e.g. Genesis 17:7–8; Leviticus 26:12; Deuteronomy 7:6; Jeremiah 11:3–5; 30:22; 31:33; Ezekiel 11:20; 2 Corinthians 6:16; Revelation 21:3). The words sum up the special relationship that God has with his people. They are the expression of a covenant or agreement of loyalty and friendship.

- This special relationship or covenant is initiated by God. It is an act of condescension on his part: he acts in grace towards us. It isn't that we are better than others; we're not! The initiative lies with God and his love.

- God decides the terms of the agreement. It isn't an agreement between equal parties. What *he* says, stands.

- The covenant that we as believers stand in with God involves the three persons of the Trinity:
  □ The Father, who gave a people to his Son and sent him into the world to save them (John 6:37–40);

☐ the Son, who is the guarantee (surety) of the covenant (Hebrews 7:22), and who fulfils the demands that the law makes on us by living a perfect life for us and dying in our place (John 10:11–18). The covenant is in fact ratified by Jesus' blood (Matthew 26:28) and he is the mediator of the covenant (Hebrews 9:14–15).

the Holy Spirit, who applies the effects of Christ's death on the cross to us (1 Corinthians 2:1–5; 1 Thessalonians 1:4–10).

● The covenant is open to *all* who repent and believe (Acts 21:38–39; Romans 10:11–13).

● God changes the hearts of those who belong to him. We find that in our inmost being we want to keep God's law (Hebrews 8:10, quoting Jeremiah 31:31).

● To be practical, what does all this mean? The covenant between God and us:
☐ *is the basis of our relationship with God.* We are no longer 'foreigners to the covenants of promise, without hope and without God in the world' (Ephesians 2:12). We are in a stable unchanging relationship with God.
☐ *gives us a promise to lay hold of* when we feel far from God. As the hymn puts it: 'His oath, His cov'nant, and blood support me in the 'whelming flood . . .'.
☐ *gives us a responsibility to live out* in our lifestyle: a life of holiness and righteousness, being faithful to our God (Luke 1:72–75).

'Those who fear God need not fear want. Through all these long years the LORD has always found meat for his own children, whether they have been in the wilderness, or by the brook Cherith, or in captivity, or in the midst of famine. Hitherto the LORD has given us day by day our daily bread, and we doubt not that He will continue to feed us till we want no more.

'As to the higher and greater blessings of the covenant

of grace, He will never cease to supply them as our case
demands. He is mindful that He made the covenant, and
never acts as if He regretted it. He is mindful of it when
we provoke Him to destroy us. He is mindful to love us,
keep us, and comfort us, even as He engaged to do. He is
mindful of every jot and tittle of His engagements, never
suffering one of His words to fall to the ground.

'We are sadly unmindful of our God, but He is graciously
mindful of us. He cannot forget His Son who is the Surety
of the Covenant, nor His Holy Spirit who actively carries
out the covenant, nor His own honor, which is bound up
with the covenant. Hence the foundation of God standeth
sure, and no believer shall lose his divine inheritance,
which is his by a covenant of salt' (Charles Spurgeon).

> My hope is built on nothing less
> Than Jesus' blood and righteousness;
> I dare not trust the sweetest frame,
> But wholly lean on Jesus' Name.
>
> *On Christ, the solid Rock, I stand;*
> *All other ground is sinking sand.*
>
> When darkness veils His lovely face,
> I rest on His unchanging grace;
> In every high and stormy gale,
> My anchor holds within the veil.
>
> His oath, His cov'nant, and blood,
> Support me in the 'whelming flood;
> When all around my soul gives way,
> He then is all my hope and stay.
>
> When He shall come with trumpet sound,
> O may I then in Him be found!
> Clothed in His righteousness alone,
> Faultless to stand before the throne.
>
> Edward Mote, 1797–1874

Conclusion

Knowing that we are in a 'covenant' relationship with God isn't meant to make us proud. Rather it should give us a deep sense of gratitude to God which is to be reflected in the way we live.

'Jesus has become the guarantee of a better covenant' (Hebrews 7:22).

4

GOD IS FAITHFUL

Key thought The fact that God has a relationship of friendship with people is a sign of his unchanging faithfulness.

Key Bible verse 'They are new every morning; great is your faithfulness' (Lamentations 3:23).

God's faithfulness

- God keeps his covenant with those who love him and keep his commands (Deuteronomy 7:9).

- God cannot lie (Numbers 23:19; Titus 1:2) or do wrong (Deuteronomy 32:4).

- God's faithfulness never fails (Psalm 33:4; 2 Timothy 2:13); it lasts for ever (Psalm 119:90; 146:6).

- God's faithfulness is:
  □ great (Lamentations 3:23),
  □ immeasurable (Psalm 36:5),
  □ unshakeable (Isaiah 54:10).

- God's faithfulness is seen in:
  □ the natural order of creation (Genesis 8:22; Jeremiah 33:20–21);
  □ the keeping of his promises (Psalm 145:13; Hebrews 10:23);
  □ his calling of us as his children and the certain completion of the work already begun in us (1 Corinthians 1:9; Philippians 1:6; 1 Thessalonians 5:23–24);

☐ his forgiveness of our sins (1 John 1:9);
☐ his help when we are tempted (1 Corinthians 10:13)
and in need (2 Thessalonians 3:3).

Our response

We don't learn about God's faithfulness in the classroom.
We can only learn theory in a classroom. It is in the 'nitty-
gritty' of life, in all its troubles, its rough and tumble, that
we prove God's faithfulness.

Our picture of God's faithfulness may need sharpening.
We may need to think long and hard about some of the
scriptures above – does God really forgive our sins? Does
he really help us when we need strength and protection?
You see, our picture of God's faithfulness may come from
our view of *human* faithfulness: perhaps the party 'faithfuls'
who staunchly support their leader at a party conference
on one occasion only to turn their backs on him or her in
later years.

Or our picture of faithfulness may come from the lack
of it in marriage. When we think of faithfulness in marriage
– staying with one's husband or wife through thick and
thin, not wandering off with another man or woman – we
begin to get a picture of someone who is dependable or
reliable: someone you can *always* count on to be there and
to help. Yes, our God is like that: completely trustworthy.

So, how are we to respond to someone like this? By
trusting God, the one who is trustworthy, by putting our
faith in him, not only once and for ever when we become
Christians, but also in the here and now: in the life of
today, in your life and mine this week, this day, this moment. When faced with something that seems impossible,
I sometimes pray something like this: 'LORD, this is where
I need your grace and your help, right here and now.'
What happens? Well, it always 'seems' that an answer is
provided – something does happen. It may be that I see
the situation in a different light, or I discover an alternative

solution, or my attitude and outlook change, or circumstances change.

We need to respond to God's faithfulness in the reality of personal faith, your faith and mine. God takes the initiative and we need to respond to him. It's always been like this. Notice that all this isn't something static; it's something growing. It's all about a relationship with God through Christ.

We begin our relationship with God when we turn to him in faith and repentance, but this relationship needs nurturing. One of the things that help it grow is reading and studying God's word; another is praying. In this way we develop our personal walk with God. I remember a few years ago having to choose a design for the cover of a book on prayer. One idea was a modern telecommunications broadcasting station: a huge dish pointing skyward. This was helpful, but it was a picture of something unmoving or static – almost clinical. Instead we chose a stream flowing down a hillside: that was where life was! (We put the picture of the telecommunications dish inside the book, so the two complemented each other.)

This is what a *covenant* (see the previous section) is all about – a relationship, a friendship: not a dry, dusty, legal agreement but the expression of an agreement in life. Take, if you will, a group of 'the lads' who play together, drink together, and joke together. They have an unwritten agreement that they 'belong' in some way to one another. And they feel let down when one of them, say, gets married or stops wanting to drink every evening with the others. There's a true network of relationships for you.

Christian communicators have sometimes given the idea that the Christian life is summed up in personal Bible reading, prayer and going to meetings. All these are important, but they're not the be-all and end-all of our Christian life. These are the *roots* of our life, a 'hidden' life under the surface; but there's a fruit above the surface, a fruit that comes about by *obedience*, by acting on God's word. Take for example the decorator who wanted to paint our house on a Sunday. My wife and I hummed and hawed and eventually told him that this went against our principles. It turned out all right; he respected our beliefs and painted the house on a weekday instead. We acted on what we believed to be right. Or take the odd occasions my wife and I went out knocking on people's doors to try to befriend them and tell them about Jesus. That took some courage, but it was putting our faith into action.

'Great is Thy faithfulness', O God my Father,
    There is no shadow of turning with Thee;
Thou changest not, Thy compassions they fail not;
    As Thou hast been Thou for ever wilt be.

'Great is Thy faithfulness! Great is Thy faithfulness!'
    Morning by morning new mercies I see!
All I have needed Thy hand hath provided –
    'Great is Thy faithfulness', Lord, unto me!

Summer and winter, and springtime and harvest,
    Sun, moon and stars in their courses above,
Join with all Nature in manifold witness
    To Thy great faithfulness, mercy and love.

Pardon for sin and a peace that endureth,
    Thy own dear presence to cheer and to guide,
Strength for today and bright hope for tomorrow,
    Blessings all mine, with ten thousand beside!

Thomas O. Chisholm, 1866–1960

Conclusion

God's faithfulness isn't just another 'attribute' of his character. He is faithful and this fact can be – and is to be – experienced in our daily lives as we depend on him.

'God, who has called you into fellowship with his Son Jesus Christ our LORD, is faithful' (1 Corinthians 1:9).

5

AMAZING GRACE!

> *Key thought* God acts in love towards us, even though we don't deserve it.
>
> *Key Bible verse* 'The God of all grace' (1 Peter 5:10).

The grace of God: Matthew 20:1–16

● Two important truths stand out in this parable: God's grace is *free* and God's grace is *sovereign*.

Notice that the landowner (clearly standing for God) was a caring person. He gave work to those who needed it. He agreed to pay the first workers a fair wage: a day's pay for a day's work.

We see that the landowner gets more and more generous as the day goes on. Each worker, regardless of how long he has worked, gets paid a day's wages. He received what he needed in order to keep his family, not what he deserved on a strict hourly rate. The landowner chose to pay them according to their need, according to grace.

Jesus pays particular attention to the group hired at the eleventh hour. How generously they were treated! They, as well as the others, needed money to support their families; the landowner saw their need and so offered them work.

God sees our need, too: how we are sinners. We need saving from condemnation and hell. The miracle of grace is that God doesn't deal with us according to what we deserve. In spite of our sin, he loves us. In love, he gave his Son to die on the cross; as the old definition puts it, *G*od's *R*iches *a*t *C*hrist's *E*xpense.

● God's grace is not only free; it is also sovereign. God has the right to choose what he wants to do (as in the parable, verse 15, 'Don't I have the right to do what I want with my own money?'). How do we react to this? How do we react when we see other Christians 'being blessed' (as we put it) by God more than we're 'blessed' (or seem to be). Are we envious because God is generous to others (verse 15)?

There's a shop in town where they seem to treat me nicely. They know my name and say hello cheerily when I go in: they make me feel important. But one day I noticed that the shop assistants act in the same way with other people as well. My reaction: I felt cheated! I wanted to be the only one who came in for special treatment! God's grace is saying that we're not to grumble (verse 11) at how others are treated. God can treat us how he wants: he is God, after all (see also Romans 9:20–21). In fact God isn't unfair to any of us (verse 13 of the parable). If he treated any of us justly, we would be condemned to hell; the wonder of mercy is that he stays his anger and the joy of grace is that he loves us in spite of our sin (Ephesians 2:1–10).

● Grace is the free gift of God, given, as God chooses, to those who deserve the opposite. It is completely undeserved by us; it depends only upon God's own will.

● As we have seen in earlier sections, God chose a people to be his own. He pledged himself to them. And he remained faithful to them even when they were unfaithful to him (Hosea 11).

● We can't do anything to put ourselves right with God (Romans 3:20). As the hymn puts it:

> Not the labours of my hands
> Can fulfil Thy law's demands;
> > Could my zeal no respite know,
> > Could my tears for ever flow,
> All for sin could not atone:
> Thou must save, and Thou alone.

- We see God's grace in our salvation:
  ☐ We are called by God's grace (Galatians 1:15).
  ☐ We are put right with God by his grace (Romans 3:24), centred on the cross (Romans 3:24–25; 5:8; Titus 3:4–7). The way we lay hold of such grace is by faith (Romans 3:25; Ephesians 2:8).

- God's grace means that he forgives our sins; he doesn't hold them against us (Psalm 103:3, 11–12; Hebrews 10:17). Note that God's grace doesn't merely cancel sin; it gives us life and salvation. What is true about sin is exceeded infinitely by what God has done by his grace through Jesus (Romans 5:20–21).

- We are kept by grace. Grace preserves us (Isaiah 49:16; John 10:27–29). As another hymn puts it:

> My name from the palms of His hands
> > Eternity will not erase;
> Impressed on His heart it remains,
> > In marks of indelible grace;
> Yes, I to the end shall endure,
> > As sure as the earnest is given;
> More happy, but not more secure,
> > The glorified spirits in heaven.

> Amazing grace (how sweet the sound)
> > That saved a wretch like me!
> I once was lost, but now am found;
> > Was blind, but now I see.

'Twas grace that taught my heart to fear,
    And grace my fears relieved;
How precious did that grace appear
    The hour I first believed!

Through many dangers, toils and snares
    I have already come;
'Tis grace has brought me safe thus far,
    And grace will lead me home.

The Lord has promised good to me,
    His Word my hope secures;
He will my shield and portion be
    As long as life endures.

Yes, when this flesh and heart shall fail
    And mortal life shall cease,
I shall possess within the veil
    A life of joy and peace.

The earth shall soon dissolve like snow,
    The sun forbear to shine;
But God, who called me here below,
    Will be for ever mine.

John Newton, 1725–1807

Conclusion

God is called 'the God of all grace' (1 Peter 5:10).
This is what the God of the promises is like.

'For it is by grace you have been saved, through faith
– and this not from yourselves, it is the gift of God –
not by works, so that no-one can boast' (Ephesians
2:8–9).

6

THE NAMES OF GOD

Key thought In the different names for God in the Bible we can see afresh that God is wholly trustworthy.

Key Bible verse 'Moses said to God, "Suppose I go to the Israelites and say to them 'The God of your fathers has sent me to you,' and they ask me, 'What is his name?' Then what shall I tell them?" ' (Exodus 3:13).

The names of God

We can distinguish three different kinds of names of God:
- the general names;
- the covenant name;
- other special names.

- The general names.
  ☐ *El.* The word means 'God' or 'god' in a wide sense. It is used especially with other descriptions of God to show his distinctive nature. For example, he is:
  almighty (Genesis 17:1; El Shaddai);
  the highest God (Genesis 14:18; El Elyon);
  eternal (Genesis 21:33; El Olam);
  the God who sees (Genesis 16:13; El Roi);
  living (Joshua 3:10);
  holy (Isaiah 5:16);
  righteous (Isaiah 45:21);
  jealous (Exodus 20:5);
  faithful (Deuteronomy 7:9);
  merciful (Deuteronomy 4:31).

☐ *Elohim*. This word occurs over 2000 times in the Bible. It's a plural word, referring to the majesty of God (compare our royal 'we') or the persons of the Trinity, e.g. Genesis 1:1–2; 26. This is God who is the God of creation and providence, the supreme God who has all the divine characteristics, in contrast to human and other created beings.

● The covenant name: *Yahweh* (Jehovah, represented in most English versions as LORD).

☐ *The background to the name*. The original Hebrew word YHWH did not contain any vowels: YHWH was regarded as too sacred to pronounce (*Adonai* – LORD – being substituted in reading). Later, the vowels of *Adonai* were combined with YHWH to give 'Jehovah'.

☐ *The meaning of the name*. The name is related to the verb 'to be', but it means more than merely 'to exist'; it's more like 'to be actively present'. The context in which this name was revealed – Exodus 3:13–16 – is significant: God showed himself as the holy one who would redeem his people. The word had been used earlier (Genesis 4:1, 26) when it seems to have been just a way of addressing God. Exodus (3:13–16; 6:2–3) shows us that Yahweh was a firm statement of the character of God: that he was holy, that he was redeemer, that he was always present with his people.

☐ *Working it out for us*. Isn't this something that we need to learn time and time again? God is always with us, whatever situation we're in. He does not change in his relationship with his people.

● Other special names.

☐ Many of these are names linked to Jehovah:
Jehovah-Jireh (the LORD will provide; Genesis 22:14), when the angel of the LORD pointed to a ram as a substitute for Isaac;
Jehovah-Nissi (the LORD is my banner; Exodus 17:15), after the defeat of the Amalekites;

Jehovah-Shalom (the LORD is peace; Judges 6:24), the name given by Gideon to an altar built to the LORD;

Jehovah-Tsidkenu (the LORD Our Righteousness; Jeremiah 23:6; 33:16);

Jehovah-Tsebahoth (Sabaoth) (the LORD Almighty; 1 Samuel 1:3; Jeremiah 32:18). Older English versions translate this 'the LORD of Hosts', the one who is sovereign over the powers in heaven and on earth;

Jehovah-Rohi (the LORD is my shepherd; Psalm 23:1; 80:1).

□ Other names include *Adonai* (Lord, e.g. with *Yahweh*: NIV 'Sovereign LORD', Genesis 15:2, 8; Exodus 23:17).

□ *Working it out*. Again, aren't these aspects of God's character that we need to remind ourselves of? When we need strength or help, *he* can provide; in conflict *he* is our banner; in turmoil and trouble, *he* is our peace; when overwhelmed by our sin, *he* is our salvation and righteousness; when Satan launches his attacks, he is our LORD Almighty; in times of danger and guidance, he is our shepherd.

From the Old Testament into the New

We cannot set the New Testament against the Old Testament. The same God speaks and reveals himself in both.

• We see God as *Father*:

□ of all the human race in creation (Malachi 2:10; Acts 17:28, 29);

□ of Christ, by eternal generation (Romans 15:6; 2 Corinthians 1:3);

□ of his people (John 1:12; 14:6; 2 Corinthians 6:18; Galatians 4:6, *Abba* is Aramaic for 'Father'; 1 John 3:1–2). Note that Jesus states that the relationship he has with his Father is different from ours with the Father (John 20:17).

• When the Old Testament was translated into Greek,

the word *kyrios* was used to translate *Yahweh*. The New
Testament was written in Greek and the same word
kyrios is translated 'Lord' in our English Bibles. The
word used for Yahweh is used for Jesus Christ! On
many occasions in the New Testament, Old Testament
passages that referred to Yahweh are applied to Christ
(Acts 2:34–35 applies Psalm 110:1; Romans 10:13
applies Joel 2:32; Philippians 2:9–11 applies Isaiah
45:23). Further, Jesus took the name of God, Yahweh (I
AM, Exodus 3:14) and applied it to himself (e.g. John
8:58, 6:35).

> The God of Abraham praise,
>> Who reigns enthroned above,
> Ancient of everlasting days,
>> And God of love.
> Jehovah! Great I AM!
>> By earth and heaven confessed;
> I bow and bless the sacred Name
>> For ever blessed.
>
> The God of Abraham praise,
>> At whose supreme command
> From earth I rise, and seek the joys
>> At His right hand.
> I all on earth forsake –
>> Its wisdom, fame, and power –
> And Him my only portion make,
>> My shield and tower.
>
> The God of Abraham praise,
>> Whose all-sufficient grace
> Shall guide me all my happy days
>> In all my ways.
> He is my faithful Friend,
>> He is my gracious God;
> And He shall save me to the end
>> Through Jesus' blood.

He by Himself hath sworn,
  I on His oath depend:
I shall, on eagles' wings upborne,
  To heaven ascend;
I shall behold His face,
  I shall His power adore,
And sing the wonders of His grace
  For evermore.

There dwells the Lord our King,
  The Lord our Righteousness,
Triumphant o'er the world and sin,
  The Prince of Peace;
On Zion's sacred height
  His kingdom He maintains,
And glorious with His saints in light
  For ever reigns.

The whole triumphant host
  Give thanks to God on high;
Hail, Father, Son, and Holy Ghost!
  They ever cry.
Hail, Abraham's God, and mine!
  I join the heavenly lays;
All might and majesty are Thine,
  And endless praise.

Thomas Olivers, 1725–99

Conclusion

No human mind can fully understand God. But in these descriptions we begin to sense something of the one who has declared himself as our Father.

' "I tell you the truth," Jesus answered, "before Abraham was born, I am!" ' (John 8:58).

7

CAN WE REALLY TRUST GOD?

Key thought The example of Abraham shows us how to lay hold of the promises of God by trusting him even when everything seems impossible.

Key Bible verse 'He [Abraham] did not waver through unbelief regarding the promise of God, but was strengthened in his faith and gave glory to God, being fully persuaded that God had power to do what he had promised' (Romans 4:20–21).

The example of Abraham

● Genesis 12:1–9.
   □ Notice the blending of commands and promises in God's call to Abram. How did Abram respond (see also Hebrews 11:8)? God called Abram to leave the busy city of Ur, and Haran, his family, his friends, his old way of life and to step out into an unknown world. 'Faith obeys God by launching out upon His promises and by doing His bidding without question' (Francis Dixon).
   □ What were the specific promises that God made to Abram (verses 2–3, 7)? Notice Abram's step-by-step practical and also spiritual response through verses 4 to 9.

● Genesis 15:1–7.
   □ In these verses, for the first time in the Bible, come four striking phrases that recur throughout the Scrip-

tures: 'the word of the LORD came' (verse 1), 'Do not be afraid' (verse 1), 'I am your shield' (verse 1), and 'believed' (verse 6).

☐ Abram had just defeated Kedorlaomer (chapter 14, especially verse 17). He was now back to everyday life and nothing of what God had foretold him was on the horizon. Notice how the promises of verse 1 relate exactly to his needs at that time.

☐ 'God does not content Himself with vague assurances. He gives us solid ground for comfort in some fresh revelation of Himself' (F. B. Meyer).

☐ How did Abram obtain the hope of having descendants in the face of circumstances that, humanly speaking, were completely hopeless? What else did God receive by his response (verse 6)? Notice how Paul refers to this with reference to the gospel (Romans 4:2–5, 13–25).

☐ God gave Abram sure grounds for his faith. Why do you think God also made a covenant with Abram (15:9–21; 17:1–27)?

● Genesis 22:1–19.

☐ Where there is true faith in God, that faith will always be tested. Yes, it is God who does the testing (verse 1). There seem to be degrees of testing. Although it was Abraham's severest test, his offer of Isaac wasn't his first test of faith; it was almost his last. Yet because Abraham had known and trusted the Lord for many years, he was ready for such a test.

☐ As Abraham thought about God's request he must have known that sacrificing Isaac would mean giving up all hope of seeing God's promises fulfilled: there would be no great nation, no promised land, no coming Saviour. Yet because God had made these promises to Abraham, insisting that these would be carried out through Isaac, Abraham had another thought: see Hebrews 11:17–18. The answer to the difficulty must be that God would raise Isaac from the dead.

☐ So it is that Abraham's faith is seen in his actions (see also James 2:20–24). And we see God's great provision (verses 11–14). This provision foreshadows the sacrifice of the Son of God (see John 3:16; 1 John 4:9–10).

The testing of our faith

How do we react when God tests our faith . . . when trusting him seems to be the last thing on earth we want to do?

● As we have seen, testing comes to us all. Why? God wants us to grow – and grow up. A young sapling grows into a sturdy mature tree by putting down roots, by growing in the face of the wind, rain and the weather. God wants his people to grow (see also John 15:1–8; 1 Peter 1:7).

● Abraham was 'called God's friend' (James 2:23). He knew God: there was a closeness between God and him. To know someone thoroughly means to trust them. As God's promises had become part of Abraham's life over the years and as God himself had become precious to Abraham, Abraham had learnt to trust the God of the promise. And Abraham didn't give up even when everything seemed impossible. How did he do this? How can we do it? 'For every look at the unlikelihood of the promise, take ten looks at the promise,' as F. B. Meyer comments. We need to think long and deep about God and his promises.

● Abraham didn't just *say* he trusted God; he acted on his professed faith as well. He obeyed (Genesis 12:4; 15:6; 22:1–11; Hebrews 11:8–13, 17–19; James 2:20–24). For us, it's all too easy to say, 'Yes, I believe,' without that faith being seen in life. In fact, at times our lives may seem to show the opposite of such faith. An important area of life regarding taking God at his word and living out our faith is in the decisions we make. Some decisions are small, such as how to spend our leisure time in the evenings or weekends. Some decisions are big, such as where to live, whom to marry, and what job to do. The way we handle these matters, and what we do, are evidence of our faith and trust in God. The example of Abraham shows that a life given back to God is one that he uses. A life lived for him is pleasing to him.

Put thou thy trust in God,
In duty's path go on;
Walk in His strength with faith and hope,
So shall thy work be done.

Give to the winds thy fears;
Hope, and be undismayed:
God hears thy sighs and counts thy tears;
God shall lift thy head.

Commit thy ways to Him,
Thy works into His hands,
And rest on His unchanging word,
Who heaven and earth commands.

Though countless years go by,
His covenant shall endure;
Though clouds and darkness hide His path,
The promised grace is sure.

Through waves and clouds and storms
His power will clear thy way:
Wait thou His time; the darkest night
Shall end in brightest day.

Leave to His sovereign sway
To choose and to command;
So shalt thou, wondering, own His way,
How wise, how strong, His hand.

Let us in life, in death,
His steadfast truth declare,

And publish with our latest breath
His love and guardian care.

Paul Gerhardt, 1607–1706
translated by John Wesley, 1703–91

Conclusion
Trusting God is at times difficult. Yet because it is part of our lives of knowing God, we come to see that it is the only way to grow in our faith.

'After this, the word of the LORD came to Abram in a vision: 'Do not be afraid, Abram, I am your shield, your very great reward'' (Genesis 15:1).

8

WORKING IT OUT

The God of the promises

What effect is our thinking about God and his promises to
have on us?

- *Our lives are encouraged.* This is our God, the holy, faithful
  one, the one who does not deal with us according to our
  sins, but according to his gracious love. He is always
  present with his people. Whatever our circumstances,
  God wants to encourage us with a fresh sense of his
  reality. He also wants us to prove him in the here and
  now, to depend on him in our lives. 'Taste and see that
  the LORD is a good; blessed is the man who takes refuge
  in him' (Psalm 34:8).

- *Our faith is challenged.* How well do we know God? We
  need to remember that knowing God is different from
  knowing *about* him. We may be fascinated by all the
  intricacies of Christian theology but scarcely know the
  Person behind it all. How deep is our personal relationship with God?

  We have the incredible privilege of knowing the living
  God. Yet this fact also places a serious responsibility on
  us. God, the all-seeing one, sees us not only when we
  are in need; he also sees us when we are in sin. He sees
  our wrong actions, wrong motives, wrong thoughts, even
  when these are concealed from everyone else. 'Nothing
  in all creation is hidden from God's sight. Everything is
  uncovered and laid bare before the eyes of him to whom
  we must give account' (Hebrews 4:13).

- *Our worship is inspired.* God is not a distant, abstract, impersonal being. He is the living one, utterly different from us, and yet also utterly close. 'Everyone was filled with awe . . . Every day they continued to meet together in the temple courts. They broke bread in their homes and ate together with glad and sincere hearts, praising God and enjoying the favour of all the people' (Acts 2:43, 46–47). That was what the first Christians were like. Does such a reverence of God inspire our worship?

'Taste and see that the LORD is good; blessed is the man who takes refuge in him' (Psalm 34:8).

Trusting Jesus

1

THE PROMISED SAVIOUR

Key thought After God's first promise of Christ (Genesis 3:15), he is never lost sight of in the Old Testament as the promised one. Someone is coming!

Key Bible verse 'For no matter how many promises God has made, they are "Yes" in Christ' (2 Corinthians 1:20).

Promise and fulfilment

There are over 300 prophecies in the Old Testament that we see are fulfilled in the New Testament in the Lord Jesus Christ. These can be grouped:

● *Christ's person and birth.*

  ☐ He is the eternal Son of God (Psalm 2:7; Proverbs 8:22–31; Matthew 16:16; 26:63–64; John 1:1–2; Colossians 1:13–19).

  ☐ He is the Son of Man (Daniel 7:13; Matthew 8:20; Mark 14:62; John 5:27).

  ☐ He is a descendant (offspring or seed) of Abraham (Genesis 22:18; Matthew 1:1; Galatians 3:16).

  ☐ He is a descendant of David (2 Samuel 7:12–13; Matthew 1:1; Luke 1:32; Romans 1:3).

☐ He would be born of a woman (Genesis 3:15; Matthew 1:18; Galatians 4:4).

☐ He would be born of a virgin (Isaiah 7:14; Matthew 1:18).

☐ He was called Immanuel ('God with us') (Isaiah 7:14; Matthew 1:22–23).

☐ He would be born at Bethlehem (Micah 5:2; Luke 2:4–6; John 7:42).

☐ He would be called out of Egypt (Hosea 11:1; Matthew 2:15).

☐ Baby boys would be killed (Jeremiah 31:15; Matthew 2:16–18).

☐ The way would be prepared for him (Isaiah 40:3; Malachi 3:1; Matthew 3:1, 3).

☐ He would be anointed with the Holy Spirit (Isaiah 11:2; 42:1; Matthew 3:16; Acts 10:38).

☐ He would be a prophet like Moses (Deuteronomy 18:15; Acts 3:22–23).

☐ He would be like, yet superior to, the priest-king Melchizedek (Psalm 110:4; Hebrews 5:6; 7:1–19).

☐ He would be God (Isaiah 9:6–7)!

● *Christ's life and work.*

☐ His ministry amongst the needy (Isaiah 61:1–2; Luke 4:16–21).

☐ His ministry in Galilee (Isaiah 9:1–2; Matthew 4:12–17, 23).

☐ His sinlessness (Isaiah 53:9; 2 Corinthians 5:21; 1 Peter 2:22).

☐ His outstanding meekness (Isaiah 42:1–4; Matthew 12:15–21).

☐ His unflagging zeal (Psalm 69:9; John 2:17).

☐ His teaching in parables (Psalm 78:2; Matthew 13:34–35).

☐ His great miracles (Isaiah 35:5–6; Matthew 11:4–6).

☐ His suffering of insults (Psalm 69:7, 9, 26; Romans 15:3).

☐ His rejection by his brothers (Psalm 69:8; John 1:11; 7:3, 5).

☐ His offence to Israel (Isaiah 8:14; Romans 9:32–33; 1 Peter 2:8).

☐ His entrance into Jerusalem (Zechariah 9:9; Matthew 21:1–11).

☐ His rejection by the Jewish rulers (Psalm 118:22–23; Matthew 21:42).

● *Christ's suffering and death.*

☐ The betrayal of Christ by a friend (Psalm 41:9; John 13:18).

☐ The falling away of the disciples (Zechariah 13:7; Matthew 26:31, 56).

☐ The selling of Christ for thirty pieces of silver (Zechariah 11:12; Matthew 26:15).

☐ The purchase of a potter's field (Zechariah 11:13; Matthew 27:7).

☐ The appointment of a successor to Judas (Psalm 109:8; Acts 1:20).

☐ The suffering of Christ (Genesis 3:15; Psalm 22:1–21; Luke 22:44; Hebrews 2:14).

☐ Christ's suffering in the place of others (Isaiah 53:4–5; Mark 10:45).

☐ Christ's silence (Isaiah 53:7; Matthew 26:63; 27:12, 14).

☐ Christ's disfigured face (Isaiah 52:14; John 19:5).

☐ The mocking, spitting, and beating of Christ (Isaiah 50:6; Matthew 26:67).

☐ The nailing of Christ to the cross (Psalm 22:16; John 19:18; 20:25).

☐ The mocking of those around (Psalm 22:7–8; Matthew 27:39–44).

☐ The abandoning of Christ by God (Psalm 22:1; Matthew 27:46).

☐ The offering of vinegar to Christ (Psalm 69:21; Matthew 27:48; John 19:28–29).

☐ The dividing of Christ's clothes (Psalm 22:18; Matthew 27:35; John 19:24).

☐ Christ's prayer for those who crucified him (end of Isaiah 53:12; Luke 23:34).

☐ The death of Christ (middle of Isaiah 53:12; Matthew 27:50).

☐ Christ's bones were not broken (Exodus 12:46; Psalm 34:20; John 19:32–36).

☐ The piercing of Christ's side (Zechariah 12:10; John 19:34, 37).

☐ The burial of Christ (Isaiah 53:9; Matthew 27:57–60).

- *Christ's resurrection, ascension, and reign.*

☐ The resurrection of Christ (Psalm 16:10; Luke 24:6; 1 Corinthians 15).

☐ The ascension of Christ (Psalm 68:18; Luke 24:51; Acts 1:9).

☐ Christ's reign in heaven (Psalm 110:1: Matthew 22:44; Acts 2:34–35; Romans 8:34).

☐ Christ brings salvation to all nations (Isaiah 11:10, 12; 42:1; Acts 10:45).

☐ Christ's just rule (Psalm 45:6–7; John 5:30; Revelation 19:11).

☐ Christ's second coming (Acts 1:11, 1 Thessalonians 4:16). See also p. 204.

☐ Christ's everlasting kingdom (Isaiah 9:7; Daniel 7:14; Luke 1:33).

> Father of mercies, in Thy Word
> What endless glory shines!
> For ever be Thy Name adored
> For these celestial lines.
>
> Here may the blind and hungry come,
> And light and food receive;
> Here shall the lowliest guest have room,
> And taste and see and live.

Here springs of consolation rise
  To cheer the fainting mind,
And thirsting souls receive supplies,
  And sweet refreshment find.

Here the Redeemer's welcome voice
  Spreads heavenly peace around;
And life and everlasting joys
  Attend the blissful sound.

O may these heavenly pages be
  My ever dear delight;
And still new beauties may I see,
  And still increasing light!

Divine Instructor, gracious Lord,
  Be Thou for ever near;
Teach me to love Thy sacred Word,
  And view my Saviour there.

Anne Steele, 1717–78

Conclusion
You cannot think about this selection of prophecies for long without realizing how the Lord Jesus Christ permeates the entire Bible. Everything points to him!

'Beginning with Moses and all the Prophets, he [Jesus] explained to them what was said in all the Scriptures concerning himself' (Luke 24:27).

2

COMING TO FAITH IN CHRIST

> *Key thought* If we want to know God personally then we will only find him through Jesus Christ.
>
> *Key Bible verse* 'Salvation is found in no-one else for there is no other name under heaven given to men by which we must be saved' (Acts 4:12).

Seeing our need

The Bible pictures our need of God in many different ways. The pictures used include the following:

- empty – hungry and thirsty for reality (Isaiah 55:1-2; John 6:35; 4:13-14; 7:37, 38);
- weary – tired of life (Matthew 11:28-29);
- blind – unable to see where we should go (Isaiah 35:5; Matthew 4:16; John 8:12);
- lost – helpless to know the way (Luke 19:10; Romans 5:6);
- poor – spiritually bankrupt (Luke 4:18; 2 Corinthians 8:9);
- ignorant – without a true understanding of God (Job 28:12-28; Proverbs 2:1-6; Matthew 11:29).

All these are, however, like symptoms of a disease. They are *signs of an illness*, not an illness itself. The Bible calls the illness *sin*. And like most diagnoses of serious illnesses, the identifying of this most basic human frailty is not popular: being called sinners hits right at our pride. But it is only when we recognize that our fundamental problem is sin that we can begin to see a way out. 'It is not the healthy who need a doctor, but the sick . . . I have not come to call the righteous, but sinners' (Jesus, in Matthew 9:12–13).

Further, we can only have a correct understanding of sin when we see God's holiness. We will only see sin in ourselves when we realize we live in the presence of a holy God (see God is special, p. 5). In contemporary Christianity, we hear a lot about God's love, but little about his holiness. Society around us and our own spiritual half-heartedness tend to soft-pedal on the teachings of God's holiness and human sinfulness, so our sinfulness seems remote.

What is sin?

In modern usage, 'sin' perhaps occurs most frequently in the somewhat old-fashioned phrase (often used humorously) *living in sin*, referring to a man and a woman who live together as if they were married, when they are not. Such a usage is a million miles away from the biblical sense of the word. Sin isn't a lapse in society's standards of sexual decency. Sin is *an offence against God*. The words used to describe sin mean:

- missing a mark or target. The target is God's glory and we have all fallen short of this mark (Romans 3:23).
- stepping over a boundary. God's standard is laid down and, rebelling against authority as we do, we think we know better and so we break his law.
- twisting of a standard. We are 'un-right' creatures, distorted and misshapen by sin.

All these words refer to God. In every case, it is God's standard that is not kept, God's law that is transgressed, God's purpose that is twisted. Sin is going against God, turning our back on him, rebelling against him. It's living for ourselves, not for the one who made us. It is living independently from him, doing what *we* want, not what he wants. And it is in the state of sin that we all naturally find ourselves.

The results of sin

- We are out of a relationship with God. Our sin is why God is unreal in our lives (Isaiah 59:2).

- We become hardened against sin. We no longer have a conscience about wrong, pride, and other matters that we euphemistically call 'weaknesses'. Sin has deceived us into a hardness of heart (Hebrews 3:13).

- We stand condemned by a holy God; we deserve his wrath (Ezekiel 18:20; John 3:18; Romans 1:18).

- We all face death (Romans 6:23). In fact, the Bible says that in our natural state, we are spiritually dead (Ephesians 2:1–5).

- We are unable to do anything about it, of ourselves (John 8:34; Romans 5:6; 8:7).

What can be done?

We have just seen that of ourselves we are utterly incapable of remedying our hopeless state. What then can be done? Is there a cure for sin? Yes! God has provided the answer in Christ. It is by means of Christ's death on the cross that our whole state is changed: 'While we were still sinners, Christ died for us' (Romans 5:8); 'This is my blood of the covenant, which is poured out for many for the forgiveness of sins' (Jesus, in Matthew 26:28); 'He himself bore our sins in his body on the tree, so that we might die to sins and live for righteousness' (1 Peter 2:24).

What must I do to be saved?

The Bible gives a number of steps to describe the way to come to know God through Jesus Christ (John 14:6; Acts 4:12).

- *Realize that this is a serious matter.* Your eternal destiny is not something light. You need to be earnest, and listen to God's promise to those who wholeheartedly seek him: 'You will seek me and find me when you seek me with all your heart. I will be found by you' (Jeremiah 29:13–14).

- *Realize your true condition.* Like the prodigal son (Luke 15:11–32), you are far away from your father (God), because of your sin (Luke 15:17–19).

- *Repent* (Acts 2:38). This means 'to do a U-turn'. You need to be truly sorry for your former way of life and to turn from your sin to God – to finish with sin (Isaiah 55:6–7; Acts 14:15; 26:18, 20). 'Repent, then, and turn to God, so that your sins may be wiped out, that times of refreshing may come from the Lord' (Acts 3:19).

- *Believe.* This means:
  □ knowing certain fundamental facts: that God is holy, that you are a sinner, that only by means of Christ's death your sins are forgiven and you are brought into a right relationship with God (Romans 3:19–28; 1 Corinthians 15:1–5).

  □ believing these facts to be true (Acts 17:2–4; 18:4, 19). These facts will make sense to you. You will be convicted – strongly persuaded – of your *own* sin (John 16:8–11; Acts 2:37).

  □ resting upon these facts. You will give up every other way of trying to be saved (Philippians 3:3–8; Titus 3:5) and personally trust the Lord Jesus Christ himself (John 1:12; 3:16; Acts 16:30–31; Galatians 2:20; 2 Timothy 1:12). He alone can save you.

Just as I am, without one plea
But that Thy blood was shed for me,
And that Thou bidd'st me come to Thee,
   O Lamb of God, I come.

Just as I am, and waiting not
To rid my soul of one dark blot,
To Thee, whose blood can cleanse each spot,
   O Lamb of God, I come.

Just as I am, though tossed about
With many a conflict, many a doubt,
Fightings and fears within, without,
   O Lamb of God, I come.

Just as I am, poor, wretched, blind:
Sight, riches, healing of the mind,
Yea, all I need, in Thee to find,
   O Lamb of God, I come.

Just as I am, Thou wilt receive,
Wilt welcome, pardon, cleanse, relieve;
Because Thy promise I believe,
   O Lamb of God, I come.

Just as I am – Thy love unknown
Has broken every barrier down –
Now to be Thine, yea, Thine alone,
   O Lamb of God, I come.

Just as I am, of that free love
The breadth, length, depth, and height to prove,
Here for a season, then above,
   O Lamb of God, I come.

Charlotte Elliott, 1789–1871

Conclusion

Only God can enable us to give up our sins and believe in Jesus. If we come to God, saying that we truly want to turn from our sins and want to believe in Jesus Christ and be saved, then he will save us.

'Come to me, all you who are weary and burdened, and I will give you rest' (Jesus, in Matthew 11:28).

A NEW CREATION

Key thought In this section we continue to see the great privileges that are ours as Christians.

Key Bible verse 'For God so loved the world that he gave his one and only Son, that whoever believes in him shall not perish but have eternal life' (John 3:16).

The importance of conversion

- Conversion is essential to salvation (Matthew 18:3).

- In conversion, repentance and faith must go together:

    To repent is to repent with faith. We turn *from* sin. But where do we turn *to*? To Christ! This is faith!

    To believe is to come to Christ for salvation. But why should we want to be saved? Because we want to end our involvement with sin. This is repentance!

    Notice how repentance and faith go together in these verses: Mark 1:15; Acts 20:21; Acts 3:19 and 4:4; Acts 10:43 and 11:18; Acts 17:30 and 17:34.

The promises are for all believers

Who are the promises of new life in Christ for? The answer: for everyone who comes, for all who have faith. 'Everyone who calls on the name of the LORD will be saved' (Joel 2:32); 'To all who received him [Jesus], to those who believed in his name, he gave the right to become children of God' (John 1:12); 'Everyone who believes in him [Jesus] receives forgiveness of sins through his name' (Acts 10:43).

Don't these verses give you assurance? If you have truly come to Christ, if you have put your whole trust in him for salvation, then the Bible says you are saved. Another verse helped me greatly when I first became a Christian: 'All that the Father gives me will come to me, and whoever comes to me I will never drive away' (John 6:37). Jesus will never reject whoever comes to him.

The activity of God

If we have truly come to Christ, then certain things have been going on in our lives. In fact, even before we came to Christ, God had already been working for us and in us.

- *God chose us.* Some people object to this teaching of 'election', but it is in the Bible.

  ☐ As part of God's purpose in Christ, his choosing was planned in eternity and made in time (Romans 8:28–30; Ephesians 1:4–5).

  ☐ God's choosing of us is not because we're in any way good or special of ourselves. It is his choice, made by his mercy and grace (Romans 9:14–16; Ephesians 2:8–9; 2 Timothy 1:9).

  ☐ This teaching does *not* go against our own human responsibility. We aren't lost or saved against our will. Those who are not called do not want to have anything to do with the gospel; those who are called do (1 Corinthians 1:18).

  ☐ If you are not yet a Christian, don't wait for some 'mystical experience'. You are *commanded* to repent and believe! If you don't, you are lost. If you do, you will be saved. This then will be evidence that you have been called.

- *God has given us a new birth.* God's calling is something that is creative. He gives us a new nature and a new will. We find that we want to do what we did not want to do before.

☐ Life is given to us, who were once spiritually dead (Ephesians 2:1–5; James 1:18; 1 Peter 1:3, 23).

☐ The new birth means the implanting of a new nature in us (2 Corinthians 5:17; Titus 3:5–6).

☐ We are given a heart that is responsive to God (Ezekiel 11:19; 36:26–27).

☐ We are drawn to the Saviour (John 6:44).

☐ The new birth ('regeneration') is brought about by the sovereign, mysterious work of God (John 3:1–15).

What follows?

Let's review our survey of God's plan of salvation:
- calling ('election');
- new birth ('regeneration');
- conversion (repentance and faith).

Let us now see what follows, once we have come to faith in Christ. The Bible says that all these are true of every believer. All believers:
- have Christ always near them (Matthew 28:20);
- have the Holy Spirit within them (Acts 2:38; Romans 8:16; 1 Corinthians 12:13);
- are declared to be in a right relationship with God (are 'justified') (Romans 3:24; 5:1, 9; 8:30);
- are reconciled to God (Romans 5:10; 2 Corinthians 5:18–20; Ephesians 2:11–18; Colossians 1:21–23);
- are forgiven, not condemned (Jeremiah 31:34; Micah 7:18–19; Acts 10:43; Romans 8:1; Ephesians 1:7);
- have the gift of eternal life (John 6:47; 17:3; Romans 6:23);
- have access into the presence of God (Romans 5:2; Ephesians 2:18; 3:12; Hebrews 10:19–22);
- are joined to Christ (are 'in Christ') (John 15:5; 2 Corinthians 5:17; Ephesians 1:1–4);

- show in their lives that sin no longer controls them (Romans 6; 1 John 3:9);
- are called the children of God (John 1:12; 1 John 3:1);
- will certainly be brought to glory (Romans 8:30).

Some practical steps

The above are great realities that are true in our spiritual lives, our relationship with God. How are these reflected in practice? Let's close this section by looking at what happened at the birth of the church in Acts 2, for it is in our association with others who have had the same experience of God that the way forward is to be found. The new believers:

- were baptized (verse 41);
- joined the church (verse 41);
- enjoyed Christian fellowship (verses 42–46) that consisted of a 'balanced diet' of teaching, fellowship, communion, and prayer and also a practical sharing;
- experienced the reality of the presence of God (verse 43);
- knew, by God's grace, continual growth in their numbers (verse 47).

To God be the glory! great things He hath done!
So loved He the world that He gave us His Son;
Who yielded His life an atonement for sin,
And opened the life-gate that all may go in.

Praise the Lord! praise the Lord! Let the earth hear His voice!
Praise the Lord! praise the Lord! Let the people rejoice!
O come to the Father through Jesus the Son:
And give Him the glory! great things He hath done!

O perfect redemption, the purchase of blood!
To every believer the promise of God;
The vilest offender who truly believes,
That moment from Jesus a pardon receives.

Great things He hath taught us, great things He hath
  done,
And great our rejoicing through Jesus the Son;
But purer and higher and greater will be
Our wonder, our transport, when Jesus we see!

Frances Jane Van Alstyne, 1820–1915

Conclusion
How great a salvation! The amazing benefits of being
new people in Christ make us deeply thankful to our
Father.

'If anyone is in Christ, he is a new creation; the old
has gone, the new has come!' (2 Corinthians 5:17)

4

THE PROMISE OF PEACE

Key thought Peace is a quality of life that we all want, yet find so hard to have. The Bible shows us the way to experience this peace.

Key Bible verse 'Therefore, since we have been justified through faith, we have peace with God through our Lord Jesus Christ' (Romans 5:1).

Peace with God

'Therefore, since we have been justified through faith, we have peace with God through our Lord Jesus Christ' (Romans 5:1). This peace is the foundation of our lives as believers. It is no mere feeling. It is a permanent state into which we as believers are brought, solely as the result of the cross. As we appropriate by faith Christ's work on the cross, so we have peace with God. This peace is a constant inner assurance that our sins are forgiven.

- We cannot achieve our own peace with God. Such a peace was made when Christ died and rose again. God himself was the one who made peace through the blood of Jesus shed on the cross (Colossians 1:20; see also Isaiah 53:4–5)

- The New Testament in fact speaks also of peace as being the person of Jesus Christ: 'He himself is our peace' (Ephesians 2:14). He removed the barrier between Jews and Gentiles that both might come near to God.

'This state of peace we are introduced into by grace was established between God, who represented the divine government and Christ who represented the offending sinner. The sin-hating God met the sin-bearing Christ at Calvary and settled, once and for all, the sin question, providing a peace that knows no change' (Herbert Lockyer).

The peace of God

'The peace of God, which transcends all understanding, will guard your hearts and your minds in Christ Jesus' (Philippians 4:7). We see from the context that such a peace will come as a result of:

- knowing the joy of the Lord in our lives (verse 4);
- showing a gentle considerate spirit to all with whom we come into contact (verse 5);
- praying constantly, particularly about the things that trouble us (verse 6).

'Peace I leave with you; my peace I give you' (Jesus, in John 14:27). It's this calm, unruffled, unflappable spirit – which was so obvious throughout Christ's life – that I want to know more of!

'All our ways we shall commit to him, all our problems leave in his hands, and rest in his peace. Unbroken contact with God, whatever happens, brings its own rewards. In times of difficulty, pain, sorrow and apprehensiveness – when it is logical to be anxious – we may nevertheless know the peace of God, which is beyond our logic. The unconquerable power of Jesus Christ will guard our hearts and minds' (Michael Perry).

Peace is part of the fruit of the Spirit (Galatians 5:22). This means that peace grows gradually, from the inside. As well as the guidelines given in Philippians 4:4–7, we are told of at least two other ways in which this peace grows:

- The more we trust God and have our minds secure on him, so will we know 'perfect peace' (Isaiah 26:3).
- The more we obey God and love his commandments, so will we have a deeper peace (Psalm 119:165).

But what is this peace? It is more than just not having a troubled feeling or fear (John 14:27). It is a quiet assurance inside us that we are believers; it is a knowledge that God is with us whatever our circumstances, 'a quiet calm and sense of well-being in the face of turmoil and tempest' (Wayne Detzler). Beautifully, such peace is Jesus' very own peace, in stark contrast to that offered by the world (John 14:27; 16:33; Matthew 11:28).

Peace from God

'Grace and peace to you from God our Father and from the Lord Jesus Christ' is the opening of Paul's letter to the Romans (Romans 1:7). It's the form of opening greeting that is found in most of his letters (and see also Numbers 6:26). As William Hendriksen comments, 'It is not the reflection of an unclouded sky in the tranquil waters of a picturesque lake, but rather the cleft of the rock in which the Lord hides his children when the storm is raging.' Peace here flows from God like a constant stream: his grace proceeds in practical ways for those who are at peace with God, and who have peace through believing.

The God of peace

God himself is described as 'the God of peace' (Hebrews 13:20), and the Lord Jesus Christ is prophesied as being the 'Prince of Peace' (Isaiah 9:6). He brought peace to the natural elements (Mark 4:39), uttered words of peace often in his life, for example Luke 7:50; 8:48; and brought peace after his resurrection (John 20:19, 21, 26). The gospel is the 'gospel of peace' (Ephesians 6:15), yet it may well bring conflict, for example in families (Matthew 10:34–36).

Making peace

But peace is not just something inward. The Christian is called on to *make* peace (Matthew 5:9; James 3:18) – to seek peace with all people (Romans 12:18; Hebrews 12:14). It is only those who really know God's peace who can resist the pressures of the world and radiate this peace to others.

- Peace is to be kept and maintained in our churches (Ephesians 4:3; Colossians 3:15). All barriers such as that between Jew and Gentile have been broken down (Ephesians 2:14, 17). And all is to be done in order, not in confusion (1 Corinthians 14:33). This thought might give more self-control and planning to some gatherings.

- But what of the world? Isn't world peace more important, someone may ask? Do we pray for world peace? And are we encouraging some Christians to play a part in bringing this about? We recognize that no organization, no agreement, nothing can ultimately change the sin of individuals' hearts – only God can – but we do have our part to play. One day peace will be known in righteousness and wholeness in the world (Isaiah 2:4; 32:17–18).

The way to find peace

True peace and rest in our lives are only to be found in the presence of God himself (Exodus 33:14; Matthew 11:28–30). Apart from him, our inner life is like a troubled sea – driven to and fro with perplexing doubts and fears. So it is that in the middle of difficulties we can have an inward peace in Christ.

- We tend to think that a lot of activity is a sign of strength, but the Bible reminds us that our strength is to be in a quiet trust and confidence in God (Isaiah 26:3; 30:15; 32:17).

- 'Be still, and know that I am God' (Psalm 46:10) is often quoted. Its various paraphrases include 'Relax – I am

the mighty one', 'Quiet! . . .', and even 'Shut up! . . .'.
These are good in that they cause me – and, hopefully,
you – to be truly still for a while in God's presence, to
draw again quietly on his infinite resources.

Peace, perfect peace, in this dark world of sin?
The blood of Jesus whispers peace within.

Peace, perfect peace, by thronging duties pressed?
To do the will of Jesus, this is rest.

Peace, perfect peace, with sorrows surging round?
On Jesus' bosom nought but calm is found.

Peace, perfect peace, with loved ones far away?
In Jesus' keeping we are safe, and they.

Peace, perfect peace, our future all unknown?
Jesus we know, and He is on the throne.

Peace, perfect peace, death shadowing us and ours?
Jesus has vanquished death and all its powers.

It is enough: earth's struggles soon shall cease,
And Jesus call us to heaven's perfect peace.

Edward Henry Bickersteth, 1825–1906

Conclusion
The one who is our peace gives peace for those who
are at peace with God.

'Peace I leave with you; my peace I give you' (Jesus,
in John 14:27).

5

THE PROMISE OF FORGIVENESS

> *Key thought* We need to know God's forgiveness in our own lives every day.
>
> *Key Bible verse* 'If we confess our sins, he is faithful and just and will forgive us our sins and purify us from all unrighteousness' (1 John 1:9).

The forgiveness of our sins: 1 John 1:5–10

Sometimes I wonder just how real we are about being Christians. We have come to Christ, we are true Christians, we carry on our lives day by day and then . . . suddenly we 'fall flat on our face', we do or say something that pulls us up with a start. Have we been play-acting, not really living out the Christian life, all along?

When we as Christians do something wrong (or neglect to do something right) – or think or speak in this way – then this is *sin*. The problem, as we have said earlier, is that this isn't a very comfortable word in our vocabulary. Even as Christians we don't like it. But it's at those times when we are aware of it that we need to do something about it – confess it (verse 9), be real with God about it, admit it, 'calling a spade a spade', and face up to it. As we confess our sin, God promises to forgive us and also to cleanse us (verse 9; see also John 13:10). But God's forgiveness isn't brought about by his 'simply waving a magic wand'. No, it cost him the life of his Son: 'It is shallow nonsense to say God forgives us because he is love. The only ground upon which God can forgive us is the cross' (Oswald Chambers). God, in his justice (verse 9 again), has paid the price of satisfying his divine anger against our sin, by causing his Son to die in our place ('propitiation', 1 John 2:2; see also Romans 3:25).

What then are the steps for us, as Christians, to know God's gift of forgiveness?

- Be serious with God about sin. It is an offence against God (Psalm 51:1–9).
- Realize that God hates sin (Habakkuk 1:13; 2 Corinthians 7:10).
- Confess – repent – talk to God and turn away from sin to God, determining, with God's help, not to sin again (Matthew 6:12; Luke 15:17–24).
- Look again long and hard at the cross where the penalty for your sin and mine was laid upon Christ (Isaiah 53:4–6).
- Receive afresh God's forgiveness and realize God no longer holds our sin against us (2 Chronicles 7:14; Psalm 32:1–5; 103:12; Hebrews 10:22).

One measure of how much we appreciate God's forgiveness is how forgiving we ourselves are towards others. Read again Jesus' telling parable in Matthew 18:21–35 and his words in Matthew 6:14–15 and Mark 11:25.

'The person who accepts forgiveness becomes deeply aware of his own weakness and need. Pride is ruled out as we take our place as supplicants before the Lord. This basic attitude releases us from our tendency to become angry with, or judgmental of, others. We begin to see others as creatures who are, like us, flawed by weakness. Rather than react with inflamed pride "He can't do this to me!", we are freed to respond as God does, with loving concern and forgiveness' (Lawrence O. Richards, *Expository Dictionary of Bible Words*).

If we really know God's forgiveness we will be amazed that God should be kind towards us. Our natural response will be love towards God (Luke 7:36–50) and kindness towards others (Luke 6:37; Ephesians 4:32; Colossians 3:13). Forgiveness means that we will give up any inward feelings of hurt, injury, or resentment towards others who have wronged us. Anger will be replaced by favour and affection. We can't do this by ourselves – we need God's grace!

- Why do you think it's difficult for us as believers to say sorry to God? How can we overcome this?
- When was the last time you truly repented of sin in your life?
- Are there people in your life whom you need to forgive?
- Spend some time thinking about the cross and the gift of Christ's forgiveness to you.

The joy of forgiveness

To summarize:
- God is the God of forgiveness (Psalm 86:5; 103:3, 12; 130:4; Isaiah 1:18).

- God alone is able to forgive sin (Isaiah 43:25; Jeremiah 31:34; Mark 2:7; Luke 5:24).

- God forgives sin through the cross (Isaiah 53:5–6; Ephesians 1:7; Colossians 1:13–14, 20; 1 Peter 2:24).

- God forgives sin on the basis of repentance and faith (Matthew 4:17; Acts 2:38, 41; Romans 3:25).

- God describes us blessed if we are forgiven (Psalm 32:1; Romans 4:7).

- God commands those who are forgiven to forgive others (Matthew 6:14–15; 18:21–22; Luke 11:4; Ephesians 4:32; Colossians 3:13).

Great God of wonders, all Thy ways
   Are matchless, godlike, and divine;
But the fair glories of Thy grace
   More godlike and unrivalled shine:

Who is a pardoning God like Thee?
Or who has grace so rich and free?

In wonder lost, with trembling joy,
   We take the pardon of our God,
Pardon for sins of deepest dye,
   A pardon sealed with Jesus' blood:

O may this strange, this wondrous grace,
   This matchless miracle of love,
Fill the wide earth with grateful praise,
   And all the angelic choirs above:

              Samuel Davies, 1723–61

Conclusion

Experiencing the forgiveness of God will lead us to a deeper worship of God, a greater sorrow for our sin, and a stronger love for other people.

'Who is a God like you, who pardons sin and forgives . . . transgression . . .?' (Micah 7:18).

6

THE PROMISE OF JESUS HIMSELF

Key thought As Christians, we know Jesus as our companion and friend. He is always near us.

Key Bible verse 'I have called you friends, for everything that I learned from my Father I have made known to you' (Jesus, in John 15:15).

Jesus is our companion

The promises of God are precious. But there is something that is even better than his promises, namely his *presence*! Whatever will happen to us, there is one who is our constant companion and friend.

- Jesus said that his Father and he would come and make their home with his disciples (John 14:23).
- He will never leave us (Matthew 28:20; Hebrews 13:5).
- We have the presence of Jesus himself along life's journey (Luke 24:15).
- We can rely on him to give help in difficulties, to give comfort in times of sorrow, and to provide strength when we are weak. He will not – he cannot – leave his own people.

Jesus is our friend

'I no longer call you servants, because a servant does not
know his master's business. Instead, I have called you
friends, for everything that I learned from my Father I
have made known to you' (Jesus, in John 15:15). What a
privilege to be in our Father's purposes!

- He is the 'friend who sticks closer than a brother' (Proverbs 18:24).
- Sometimes the love of a true friend means hurt (Proverbs
17:17; 27:6).
- Do you realize that Jesus is our friend right here and
now? We may have many earthly friends – or very few
– yet we have him. Everything that he is and has is ours,
as his friends. How tragic it is when we, rather than
cultivate our friendship with Jesus, court the friendship
of the world (James 4:4).

The secret of true friendship

If we are the friends of our God, then we stand in the
company of others, including:

- Abraham (2 Chronicles 20:7; Isaiah 41:8; James 2:23);
- Moses (Exodus 33:11).

What is the secret of true friendship? The Bible's answer
is *obedience*:

- 'You are my friends if you do what I command' (Jesus,
in John 15:14; see also John 14:23).
- We are to have a reverence for God (Psalm 25:14), taking
him at his word (James 2:23).

> When we walk with the Lord,
> In the light of His Word,
>   What a glory He sheds on our way!
> While we do His good will,
> He abides with us still,
>   And with all who will trust and obey!

But we never can prove
The delights of His love
   Until all on the altar we lay;
For the favour He shows,
And the joy He bestows,
   Are for those who will trust and obey.

Then in fellowship sweet
We will sit at His feet,
   Or we'll walk by His side in the way;
What He says we will do,
Where He sends we will go –
   Never fear, only trust and obey!

The 'crunch' is that you and I need to obey God. It is only then that we will experience a *deeper* friendship with Jesus. Are there things in your life and mine that are not given over to Jesus? Are there things that we're holding back from doing? And are we doing wrong rather than right somewhere in our lives? At work? At home?

The depth of Christ's friendship

'Greater love has no-one than this, that he lay down his life for his friends' (Jesus, in John 15:13). Jesus voluntarily gave up his own life for his friends. Such was the depth of his love (John 13:1). In a way, we can understand this: a true friend is prepared to sacrifice his life for one for whom he has true affection. But the great wonder is that our heavenly friend died on the cross for his *enemies*. Listen to the apostle: 'When we were God's enemies, we were reconciled to him through the death of his Son' (Romans 5:10; see also Philippians 3:18). How amazing it is that we may call him our friend! As Richard Baxter put it, 'Oh, that we could always think of God as we do of a friend; as of one who unfeignedly loves us, even more than we do ourselves; whose very heart is set upon us to do us good.'

The best of friends

I wonder if we have really grasped the full realization of 'Immanuel' – God with us (Matthew 1:23). He is with us in *all* our daily life.

- He is our Saviour, to deliver us from our sin (Matthew 1:21; John 3:17; Acts 4:12).

- He is our guide, to direct our way (John 10:27; 16:13; see also Psalm 32:8; Isaiah 58:11).

- He is the one who cares for us (Matthew 11:28–30; 1 Peter 5:7; see also Psalm 55:22).

- He is the one who strengthens us (2 Corinthians 12:9; Ephesians 6:10; see also Isaiah 40:29–31).

- When we go through difficult times, we will draw nearer to him. Days when he seems remote, perhaps days of loneliness or bereavement, will test our faith. Yet, he is still with us in such periods.

- On days of great joy, we can share our happiness with our best friend. And on days when we are just plodding along, carrying on as usual, he is still with us, even in the seeming monotony of our ordinary tasks.

- At times of great temptation, the thought that our friend is always near us will help us. We will know that he is watching . . . and so we shouldn't do what is in our minds.

> I've found a Friend, O such a Friend!
>   He loved me ere I knew Him;
> He drew me with the cords of love,
>   And thus He bound me to Him;
> And round my heart still closely twine
>   Those ties which nought can sever;
> For I am His, and He is mine,
>   For ever and for ever.

I've found a Friend, O such a Friend!
　　He bled, He died to save me;
And not alone the gift of life,
　　But His own self He gave me.
Nought that I have mine own I'll call,
　　I'll hold it for the Giver;
My heart, my strength, my life, my all
　　Are His, and His for ever.

I've found a Friend, O such a friend!
　　All power to Him is given,
To guard me on my onward course,
　　And bring me safe to heaven.
The eternal glories gleam afar,
　　To nerve my faint endeavour;
So now to watch! to work! to war!
　　And then – to rest for ever.

I've found a Friend, O such a Friend.
　　So kind, and true, and tender!
So wise a Counsellor and Guide,
　　So mighty a Defender!
From Him who loves me now so well
　　What power my soul can sever?
Shall life or death, or earth or hell?
　　No! I am His for ever.

James Grindlay Small, 1817–88

Conclusion
We will experience a growing friendship with Jesus
the more we follow him and do what he wants.

'All authority in heaven and on earth has been given
to me. Therefore go and make disciples of all nations
. . . And surely I am with you always, to the very end
of the age' (Jesus, in Matthew 28:18–20).

7

FOLLOWING JESUS

> *Key thought* A Christian disciple is someone who responds to the call of the Lord Jesus Christ by following him completely.
>
> *Key Bible verse* 'Follow me' (Jesus, in Luke 9:59).

True discipleship

True discipleship involves:
- counting the cost.
  - ☐ When crowds followed Jesus, he pointed out that there was a great cost in becoming a disciple (Luke 14:25–38). Following Jesus means changing established loyalties to your family and even to yourself. It involves a sacrifice – one that is too much for some (Luke 18:18–23). It is also bound to lead to some suffering (Luke 9:23). 'When Jesus tells you to take up your cross daily, he is not telling you to find some way to suffer daily. He is simply giving forewarning of what happens to the person who follows him' (John White).

- setting new priorities.
  'Follow me,' Jesus said (Luke 9:59). This means:
  - ☐ not looking back (Luke 9:62; 17:32). It's impossible to look at the one we're following, if we're constantly looking back and are preoccupied all the time with our old way of life.
  - ☐ giving up the right to choose our own way of life (Luke

9:23–24). This is one of those 'crunch' points. Who is ruling our lives? Whom do we serve? If we really are serious about following Jesus, then we will have to say 'no' to ourselves. Our ambitions, our personal comfort for example, have to stop being number one in our lives. And it is only when we have accepted the principle of dying to self that there is a real readiness to suffer persecution (Matthew 5:10–12).

☐ finishing with sin in our lives. We're called upon to do all in our power to put to death all sin in our lives, remembering that God by his Holy Spirit is helping us (Romans 8:13).

☐ becoming like Jesus (Matthew 10:25). A good test of how we're getting on is to read through the beatitudes (Matthew 5:3–10).

☐ recognizing Jesus is Lord by obeying him (Matthew 7:21, 24–27). It isn't enough to read (or write!) books like this one and to listen to sermons. The word has got to be put into practice in our lives (Luke 8:21).

☐ loving our God and our neighbour (Matthew 22:36–39) – a love that goes beyond ordinary human standards (Matthew 5:46–47).

☐ living as faithful witnesses to Jesus (Luke 24:48; Acts 1:8).

☐ being fruitful (John 15:5–8; Galatians 5:22–23).

How are you doing?

Perhaps all this talk of discipleship sounds rather extreme. It's certainly *radical*. We can't serve two masters (Matthew 6:24; Luke 16:13). It's got to be either Jesus or something else – it's impossible to have two 'number ones' in our lives.

Most of us plod on most of the time. So let's be honest. When was the last time you and I did something radically different for Jesus? If you're anything like me, perhaps not too recently. We may be more aware of our failures than our successes. I do recall an incident that is perhaps worth sharing. We were on the motorway on a Saturday and our car broke down. We were waiting round at the motorway service station for the car to be repaired. The only trouble was that lots of other people were waiting, too, for their cars to be repaired. Then it occurred to me: I'd been thinking about myself all the time – but what about the guy mending all our cars? He'd been at this job for ages. So, thinking, I suppose, 'What would Jesus do?', I offered to get him a hamburger from the take-away. Surprised, he accepted gratefully!

But to return to our failures. We're in good company (if that helps). The first disciples:

- didn't always understand what Jesus said (Mark 9:30–32; John 12:16; 20:9);
- didn't always use the power that was theirs (Mark 9:14–18);
- failed Jesus at the crucial time (Matthew 26:40–45, 69–75; Mark 14:50).

We need to remember that a disciple is a learner. So learning will mean failing at times as well as succeeding.

Promises of encouragement

The idea of 'taking up our cross daily' probably makes us afraid. In ourselves, we shy away from giving up the rights to *our* lives (as we put it). But we forget that Jesus knows us – he's sympathetic and caring. This doesn't mean he 'moves the goalposts' by lowering his demands and standards, but that he *is* near us. He wants to encourage us to move on to a closer walk with him. What promises does he give us to help us?

- Through following Jesus we will know the joy of an effective, growing Christian life (John 12:24–26; 15:2).

- The way of discipleship will mean that our lives will be saved, not lost (Luke 9:24). As we give ourselves to Jesus and 'one of the least of his brothers' (Matthew 25:40) we will be saved. The opposite course of action is to turn in on ourselves and try to hang on to all our earthly treasures. This way ends in disaster (Luke 9:25).

● As we deny ourselves because of our devotion to Jesus, we will find our true selves (Matthew 10:39). Do you remember how in the film *Chariots of Fire* Eric Liddell said he felt God's pleasure when he was running? He had given himself back to God, and he knew that his true self was being realized.

● The promise of a future glory will immeasurably make up for all the difficulties we may experience here and now (Luke 18:29–30; Romans 8:18–19; 2 Corinthians 4:17–18). Those who acknowledge him now, Jesus will acknowledge later before his Father (Matthew 10:32).

> O the bitter shame and sorrow,
> That a time could ever be,
> When I let the Saviour's pity
> Plead in vain, and proudly answered,
> 'All of self, and none of Thee!'
>
> Yet He found me; I beheld Him
> Bleeding on the accursed tree,
> Heard Him pray, 'Forgive them, Father!'
> And my wistful heart said faintly –
> 'Some of self, and some of Thee.'
>
> Day by day His tender mercy,
> Healing, helping, full, and free,
> Sweet and strong, and, ah! so patient,
> Brought me lower, while I whispered,
> 'Less of self, and more of Thee.'
>
> Higher than the highest heavens,
> Deeper than the deepest sea,
> Lord, Thy love at last hath conquered;

Grant me now my supplication –
'None of self, and all of Thee.'

Theodore Monod, 1836–1921

Conclusion

Following Jesus on his terms is costly. But not to follow him on his terms is even more costly.

'If anyone would come after me, he must deny himself and take up his cross daily and follow me. For whoever wants to save his life will lose it, but whoever loses his life for me will save it' (Jesus, in Luke 9:23–24).

8

WORKING IT OUT

Jesus lives in us

Jesus Christ, by his Spirit, lives in the hearts and lives of all believers (Galatians 2:20; Colossians 1:27). What does this mean for us? We can see here:

● *The miracle of life.*

Have we really grasped the wonder of this miracle? The Son of God, Jesus, is more than *near* us; he actually lives within us! So he's our closest companion, always with us. In some ways, then, we don't need to ask him to be near us – since he already is. (When we do ask him to be near us, we're reaffirming our dependence on him.) What an assurance it is to know that Jesus is always there to listen to us and to help us in all life's situations! Yet how slow we are to go to him in prayer when things get on top of us!

● *The challenge of obedience.*

One of the longings of the apostle Paul was that the believers in Galatia would show more of Christ in their lives: 'My dear children, for whom I am again in the pains of childbirth until Christ is formed in you' (Galatians 4:19). Christ's life is to be revealed in our mortal bodies (2 Corinthians 4:11). It is only by obedience – putting God's word into action day by day – that the reality of our faith is seen in our lives. After all, God's rule (his kingdom) is within us (Luke 17:20–21; Romans 14:17). Are we growing, not only in our understanding, but also in our acting on God's word (James 1:22)?

- *A glorious hope.*

   'Christ in you, the hope of glory' run the words of Colossians 1:27. Christ in us is the certain reason (in the Bible, 'hope' means a certainty) for expecting a future glory. One day we will see the glory of God in Christ (John 17:24), a vision that has its beginnings on earth (2 Corinthians 3:18), and reaches its peak in heaven. What a joy to look forward to!

'Christ in you, the hope of glory' (Colossians 1:27).

Growing in the Spirit

1

THE PROMISED SPIRIT

> *Key thought* The Holy Spirit is the third person of the Trinity. He now comes to all believers as our 'Counsellor'.
>
> *Key Bible verse* 'I will ask the Father, and he will give you another Counsellor to be with you for ever' (Jesus, in John 14:16).

In the past

The Holy Spirit has always been active. He was at work in creation (Genesis 1:2). He came upon some people in the Old Testament times, enabling them to do what they normally couldn't. For example, we can see the Spirit associated with the following:

- Israel's elders (Numbers 11:17–29);
- the *judge* Gideon (Judges 6:34);
- *King* Saul (1 Samuel 10:5–10);
- the *priest* Zechariah (2 Chronicles 24:20);
- the *prophet* Ezekiel (Ezekiel 2:2).

What were the activities that the Spirit carried out? In the Old Testament we see the Spirit active in:

- creation (Genesis 1:2);

- revealing God's truth and will (Numbers 24:2; 2 Samuel 23:2);
- evoking a personal response to God (Psalm 51:10–12; Ezekiel 36:25–27);
- equipping individuals for leadership (1 Samuel 16:13);
- equipping individuals with skill and strength for creative work (Exodus 31:1–5).

(Adapted from J. I. Packer, *Keep In Step With the Spirit.*)

The promise of the Spirit

There are two ways in which the Spirit and the age of the Messiah are linked:

- The coming Messiah was himself to be anointed by the Spirit (Isaiah 11:2; 42:1; 61:1; Luke 4:16–20). It was at Jesus' baptism that 'the Holy Spirit descended on him in bodily form like a dove' (Luke 3:22). The divine anointing was a necessary preparation for the work before him (Matthew 12:28; Acts 4:27; 10:38).

- In the age of the Messiah, the Spirit of God would be given in a different way and degree (Ezekiel 36:27; Joel 2:28; Acts 2:16–21). The Holy Spirit was to be a gift to *all* believers, not just special people (Acts 10:44–48).

It was after Jesus' death, resurrection, and ascension (John 7:39) that the prophesied baptism with the Holy Spirit (Matthew 3:11) happened. Acts 1:4–5 and 2:33 show us that this baptism with the Holy Spirit happened at Pentecost.

Jesus himself promised 'another Counsellor' (John 14:16). (Other translations for 'Counsellor' include: Comforter, Strengthener, Helper, Advocate, Ally, Adviser, and senior Friend.) The Holy Spirit is the one who comes alongside us to help us. He is the one who carries on the ministry of Jesus. The Holy Spirit would come from the Father and the Son (Luke 24:49; John 14:26; 15:26; 16:7).

Who is the Spirit?

In the New Testament, the Holy Spirit is seen as the third person of the Trinity.

- He is a person. He is referred to as *he*, not *it* (John 14:17; 15:26; 16:7–8). The actions of the Holy Spirit include his:
  - ☐ searching (1 Corinthians 2:10),
  - ☐ determining (1 Corinthians 12:11),
  - ☐ hearing (John 16:13),
  - ☐ speaking (Acts 8:29; 13:2; 1 Timothy 4:1; Revelation 2:7),
  - ☐ calling out (Galatians 4:6),
  - ☐ praying (Romans 8:26),
  - ☐ bearing witness (John 15:26; Romans 8:16),
  - ☐ revealing (John 16:14–15),
  - ☐ teaching (John 14:26),
  - ☐ commanding (Acts 16:6–7),
  - ☐ convicting (John 16:7–15),
  - ☐ guiding (John 16:13),
  - ☐ leading (Romans 8:14; Galatians 5:18),
  - ☐ bringing glory to Christ (John 16:14),
  - ☐ raising from the dead (Romans 8:11),
  - ☐ giving speech (Acts 2:4),
  - ☐ giving help (Romans 8:26),
  - ☐ moving (Acts 8:39),
  - ☐ being lied to (Acts 5:3–4),
  - ☐ being grieved (Ephesians 4:30),
  - ☐ being tested (Acts 5:9),
  - ☐ being resisted (Acts 7:51),
  - ☐ being insulted (Hebrews 10:29),
  - ☐ being blasphemed against (Matthew 12:31).

  The Holy Spirit is not a mere impersonal force, an *it*; he is a *he*, a person of the Trinity.

- He is God.
  - ☐ The Spirit is described as God. In a number of instances, a combination of passages emphasizes the

equality of the persons in the Trinity. For example, Isaiah 6:8–9. Isaiah hears the Lord saying, 'Whom shall I send . . .?' Later, Isaiah is commissioned to be a prophet with the words, 'Go and tell this people . . .'. When Paul quotes these words in Acts 28:25–27 he says that it was the Holy Spirit speaking. Similar groups of passages include: Exodus 17:7, Psalm 95:8, and Hebrews 3:7–11 ('the Holy Spirit says', verse 7); Jeremiah 31:31–34 and Hebrews 10:15–16.

☐ The Spirit has the characteristics of God. The Holy Spirit is eternal (Hebrews 9:14). He is everywhere all the time (Psalm 139:7–10). He knows everything (Isaiah 40:13–14; 1 Corinthians 2:10–11). He can do all he wants to (1 Corinthians 12:11).

☐ The works of God are described as being the work of the Holy Spirit. God is the creator; yet the Holy Spirit is also Creator (Job 33:4). God works miracles; so does the Holy Spirit (Matthew 12:28; 1 Corinthians 12:9–11). God gives the new birth, by the Holy Spirit (John 3:5–6). Who but God can bring the dead back to life (Romans 8:11)? Who apart from God could gradually change the character of believers to be more like God (2 Corinthians 3:18)? Who could be the author of the Scriptures, except God (2 Timothy 3:16; 2 Peter 1:21)? Only God can do these works of God. And exactly these are the works of the Holy Spirit.

☐ Worship – which is only to be rendered to God – is made to the Holy Spirit. Those who are baptized are baptized in his name ('in the name of the Father and of the Son and of the Holy Spirit', Matthew 28:19). It is possible to blaspheme against God, the Holy Spirit (Matthew 12:31–32). And Paul calls on the Holy Spirit when he prays the blessing of the three-in-one God on his readers in Corinth (2 Corinthians 13:14).

Come down, O Love divine,
Seek Thou this soul of mine,

And visit it with Thine own ardour glowing;
O Comforter, draw near,
Within my heart appear,
   And kindle it, Thy holy flame bestowing.

O let it freely burn,
Till earthly passions turn
   To dust and ashes, in its heat consuming;
And let Thy glorious light
Shine ever on my sight,
   And clothe me round, the while my path illuming.

Let holy charity
Mine outward vesture be.
   And lowliness become mine inner clothing;
True lowliness of heart,
Which takes the humbler part,
   And o'er its own shortcomings weeps with loathing.

And so the yearning strong,
With which the soul will long,
   Shall far outpass the power of human tellingg;
For none can guess its grace,
Till he become the place
   Wherein the Holy Spirit makes His dwelling.

Bianco da Siena, *c.* 1350–1434
tr. by Richard Frederick Littledale, 1833–90

Conclusion
Although Jesus is no longer physically present with us, the Spirit is present with all of God's people. Christ now comes to us by the Spirit. So in having the Holy Spirit, we have Christ himself.

'And I will put my Spirit in you and move you to follow my decrees and be careful to keep my laws' (Ezekiel 36:27).

2

THE ACTIVITY OF THE SPIRIT

Key thought The main work of the Spirit is to point us to the Lord Jesus Christ.

Key Bible verse 'The Spirit of Jesus' (Acts 16:7).

'Take courage!'

As I sit here and write these words, I confess I am afraid – afraid of the work of the Holy Spirit. A friend who has recently become a Christian described some of the manifestations of the Spirit as 'weird'. As Christian believers, there are some who are afraid, while others 'take in their stride' the moving of the Holy Spirit.

How can the fears of some of us be allayed? By remembering who the Spirit is:

- He is the Spirit of Jesus (Acts 16:7), the Spirit of Christ (Romans 8:9). The relationship between the Spirit and our Saviour is intimate and almost indissoluble. The work of the Spirit cannot be separated from the work of Christ. 'Remember that the Spirit is the Spirit of Jesus, who is gentle and loving and wants the very best for our lives' (Michael Green).

- He is the Spirit of truth (John 14:17, 15:26, 16:13). He is the truth in person and he leads God's people into that truth. Do I want to know God's right way to live in the world? If so, then I need to follow the Spirit of truth (remembering of course that the Spirit inspired the writers of the Scriptures).

● He is the Spirit of sonship: 'For you did not receive a spirit that makes you a slave again to fear, but you received the Spirit of sonship' (Romans 8:15). This is a basic ministry of the Holy Spirit: he reminds us that we really are God's children (Romans 8:16). It is this Spirit who lives in me (Romans 8:9). It is this Spirit who has come alongside me – now (John 14:16). I am reminded that I should fight any tendencies towards being afraid. The Holy Spirit isn't 'a spirit of timidity', but a spirit of power, of love and of self-discipline' (2 Timothy 1:7). How we need power and love, exercised in a self-controlled way!

As Bruce Milne writes in *Know the Truth*, 'Alarm at an *authentic* ministry of the Spirit needs the reassurance the disciples received when they saw Jesus walking on the sea of Galilee and cried out for fear it was a ghost, "Take courage! It is I. Don't be afraid" ' (Matthew 14:26–27).

The work of the Spirit

The main work of the Spirit is to point to Jesus: 'He will bring glory to me by taking from what is mine and making it known to you' (Jesus, in John 16:14). Jim Packer most helpfully calls this 'a floodlight ministry'. Floodlights are placed in such a position that they are hidden: their task is simply to shine onto a building. So it is with the Holy Spirit: he is, as it were, 'the hidden floodlight shining on the Saviour'. The Holy Spirit's role is a self-effacing one: he does not point to himself but to Jesus. How, then, is this work of the Spirit seen?

● The Spirit brings home to the world what it means to reject Jesus. He convicts of the sin of not believing in Christ, Christ's righteousness – because Christ went in

victory over death to the Father – and of God's judgment
on Satan (John 16:8–11).

- The Spirit gives new birth (John 3:5–6; Titus 3:5). (See
  also p. 44).

- The Spirit lives in all believers. The gift of the Holy
  Spirit remains permanently in all Christians (John
  14:16–17; Acts 2:38; Romans 8:9; 1 Corinthians 3:16).

- All believers are sealed with the Holy Spirit (Ephesians
  1:13–14; 4:30). When we believe, we are 'marked
  people', spiritually speaking. The Holy Spirit identifies
  us as God's own people. We are genuinely his! And
  the Holy Spirit is the certain, secure deposit (the first
  instalment or introduction, older versions had 'earnest')
  of our future inheritance (2 Corinthians 1:22).

- The Spirit makes Christ real to believers. He applies the
  effects of Christ's death, resurrection, and present life to
  us. (Read through Romans 8 again slowly, applying it
  to yourself.)

- Believers are baptized with (or in or by) the Holy Spirit.
  There are different understandings as to what this
  means. Is the baptism with the Spirit an aspect of what
  it means to become a Christian or something that happens as a distinct experience after becoming a Christian?
  There are seven biblical references to being baptized
  with the Holy Spirit. Six, for example Matthew 3:11,
  refer to John the Baptist's contrast between his prepara-
  tory ministry – baptizing with water – and Jesus' ministry – baptizing with the Holy Spirit. The other reference,
  1 Corinthians 12:13, describes the unity of the experience
  of the Spirit of all believers. My understanding of these
  Scriptures, together with the general teaching on baptism, is that 'baptism with the Spirit' is an aspect of
  what it means to become a Christian. 'It highlights what
  regeneration implies, entry into the promised Messianic

Kingdom through immersion into the life of the Holy Spirit . . . "Baptism in the Spirit" is therefore one of the ways the New Testament speaks about "becoming a Christian" ' (Bruce Milne).

● Believers are to be filled with the Spirit. The command comes in Ephesians 5:18: 'Be filled with the Spirit.' Notice this is:

☐ a command. In other words, as believers, we're not just to sit around waiting for this to happen. We are responsible for doing something.

☐ in the plural. In American English the wording would be '*You all* be filled with the Spirit'. It's up to *all* of us! Wow! Just think what could happen if we really had Spirit-filled churches!

☐ in the passive. This means that something *has to be done to us* rather than us doing anything. We need to allow the Holy Spirit to fill us.

☐ in the present tense. So it means: be *continually* filled. Being filled with the Spirit isn't a one-off event. It wasn't in New Testament times (see Luke 1:15, 41, 67; 4:1; Acts 2:4; 4:8, 31; 6:3; 7:55; 9:17; 13:9). Don't you and I have a need to go on and on being filled with God himself?

Being filled with the Spirit means that the Holy Spirit will affect the way we live. He will be the main factor in our lives. Moment by moment we need to come under his influence. Sometimes we will be enabled (i.e. he will enable us) to do things that are particular signs of his reality in us: look again, for example, at Acts 4:31. Generally, our lifestyle will be different: look again at the verses surrounding the command in Ephesians 5:18, for example verses 15–33 of chapter 5. The marks of our being filled with the Spirit are essentially our becoming like Christ and God (Ephesians 5:1).

> Breathe on me, Breath of God;
> Fill me with life anew,

That I may love what Thou dost love,
   And do what Thou wouldst do.

Breathe on me, Breath of God,
   Until my heart is pure,
Until with Thee I will one will,
   To do and to endure.

Breathe on me, Breath of God,
   Till I am wholly Thine,
Until this earthly part of me
   Glows with Thy fire divine.

Breathe on me, Breath of God;
   So shall I never die,
But live with Thee the perfect life
   Of Thine eternity.

                              Edwin Hatch, 1835–89

Conclusion

It is vital that we do not neglect the continuing work of the Holy Spirit in our lives.

'He will bring glory to me' (Jesus, talking about the Holy Spirit in John 16:14).

THE HELP OF THE SPIRIT

Key thought As Christians we depend on the Holy Spirit to help us live the Christian life.

Key Bible verse 'For you did not receive a spirit that makes you a slave again to fear, but you received the Spirit of sonship' (Romans 8:15).

The Spirit helps us be sure that we are Christians

God wants us to be sure that we are Christians. He wants us to be able to draw near to him 'with a sincere heart in full assurance of faith' (Hebrews 10:22). Is it presumptuous to say that we are the children of God, to say that certainly we are going to heaven? Or is this the right of every child of God?

Being sure ('assurance') of our faith, being sure that we are Christians, comes about through the means of the Holy Spirit and the Scriptures (Romans 8:16; 1 John 5:13).

What are some of the marks of being a Christian? We can gain a glimpse of these as we look at 1 John. True Christians:

- love God's commandments and make an honest attempt to keep them (1 John 2:3–5). Being a Christian does not mean that we are sinless (1:8–10), but that we cannot go on sinning carelessly (3:9). He really want to be free from sin; this is a sign of God working in us.

- love other Christians (3:14). Believing in Jesus and

loving our spiritual brothers and sisters go together (3:23).

• believe the truth about Jesus Christ: that he is the Son of God (5:1, 13).

If we genuinely can see that these facts are true of us, then we can be sure that we have eternal life (2:3; 3:14; 4:2). We are being led by the Spirit of God (Romans 8:14).

Do you see? 'How great is the love the Father has lavished on us, that we should be called children of God! And that is what we are!' (1 John 3:1) Take time to allow the Spirit to apply these truths to your heart and mind. The Holy Spirit also wants to witness directly within us (Romans 5:5; 8:16; Galatians 4:6). He wants you to be sure that you are God's child, that you can be at perfect peace in your relationship with him because Christ died for your sins. 'You can be a Christian without having assurance. But God wants you to have assurance, so pray earnestly for it. Be satisfied with nothing less than full assurance. Do not let Satan rob you of this' (Peter Jeffery).

The Spirit helps make truth known to us

Look up John 16:12–15. Jesus is saying, 'When he, the Spirit of truth, comes, he will guide you into all truth . . . He will bring glory to me by taking from what is mine and making it known to you.' What did Jesus mean by 'what is mine'? As J. I. Packer writes: 'He must have meant, at least, "everything that is real and true about me as God incarnate, as the Father's agent in creation, providence and grace, as this world's rightful lord, and as the one who actually is master of it whether men acknowledge me or not." But surely he also meant, "all that is real and true about me as your divine lover, your mediator, your surety in the new covenant, your prophet, priest and king, your Saviour from the guilt and power of sin and from the world's corruptions and the devil's clutches; and all that is true of me as your shepherd, husband, and friend, your life and your hope, the author and finisher of your faith, the lord of your own personal history, and the one who will some day bring you to be with me and share my glory, who am thus both your path and your prize". So the words "what is *mine*" come to mean "what is *yours*, by virtue of my relationship to you and yours *to me*".'

And whom did Jesus mean when he said he would 'make it known to you' (John 16:14)? It was primarily to the apostles – they received direct revelations – but also to all believers. The Spirit teaches us all truth (John 14:26). He inspired the writing of the Scriptures (2 Timothy 3:16; 2 Peter 1:21), and he is also the one who shows us their meaning. Without his help, the Bible remains a closed book. I'm sure we've all known times when reading the Bible that the truth of the Scriptures has dawned on us in a fresh way and we have sensed again the reality of God's word for ourselves.

The Spirit helps us in our praying

Here are some practical words of David Watson:
'If you find prayer dull and difficult, be still before God. Find that position of peace and rest. Shut the door on the outside world. Then specifically ask for the Holy Spirit's help and guidance. We are to learn to "pray at all times in the Spirit, with all prayer and supplication" (Ephesians 6:18). Hoist your sails! After that, launch out, trusting that the Spirit will give you increasing joy and liberty. As in the area of temptation and victory, it is a very good practice to begin with a "sacrifice of praise", whether you feel like it or not. Read a psalm of praise; sing a hymn or a chorus of praise. Worship the Lord. Fix your mind on him, his glory and majesty, his beauty and strength. "One thing have I asked of the LORD, that will I seek after; that I may dwell in the house of the LORD all the days of my life, to behold the beauty of the LORD, and to inquire in his

temple" (Psalm 27:4). "Worthy art thou, our Lord and
God, to receive glory and honour and power . . ." (Revelation 4:11). As we praise and worship like this, our vision of
him brightens, our faith grows, and prayer at once becomes
more meaningful. Dull prayer is usually rushed prayer: we
rush into God's presence and ask for this and that. But
God will not respond to our haste. He waits for our love
and adoration, so that he might pour his love into our
hearts through the Holy Spirit. Only then do we really
begin to communicate. Confession, supplication – all these
will follow as we consciously seek his face' (from *One in the
Spirit*).

Turn now to Romans 8:26–27. We *are* weak in prayer
and at certain times we just don't know what to pray. (At
other times, we do and we know we can always pray in
accordance with clear biblical principles.) The Bible text
says that at the times that we are perplexed, God's Spirit
helps us. (For example, see 2 Corinthians 12:7–10.) The
Holy Spirit is within us and he utters inexpressible groans
that express his intercession for us. And *these* intercessions
are according to God's will. The Spirit is our help!

> Father of everlasting grace,
> Thy goodness and Thy truth we praise,
>   Thy goodness and Thy truth we prove;
> Thou hast, in honour of Thy Son,
> The gift unspeakable sent down,
>   The Spirit of life, and power, and love.
>
> Send us the Spirit of Thy Son,
> To make the depths of Godhead known,
>   To make us share the life divine;
> Send Him the sprinkled blood to apply,
> Send Him our souls to sanctify,
>   And show and seal us ever Thine.
>
> So shall we pray, and never cease,
> So shall we thankfully confess

Thy wisdom, truth, and power, and love;
With joy unspeakable adore,
And bless and praise Thee evermore,
    And serve Thee as Thy hosts above:

Till, added to that heavenly choir,
We raise our songs of triumph higher,
    And praise Thee in a bolder strain,
Out-soar the first-born seraph's flight,
And sing, with all our friends in light,
    Thy everlasting love to man.

Charles Wesley, 1707–88

Conclusion
The Holy Spirit encourages us to be confident, yet humble in our walk with God.

'The Spirit helps us in our weakness' (Romans 8:26).

4

GROWING LIKE JESUS

> *Key thought* The Holy Spirit wants to make us 'holy' –
> people who show the love and goodness of God to the
> world around us.
>
> *Key Bible verse* 'Christ loved the church and gave him-
> self up for her to make her holy, cleansing her by the
> washing with water through the word, and to present
> her to himself as a radiant church, without stain or
> wrinkle or any other blemish' (Ephesians 5:25–27).

The priority of holiness

Why do you think God made you and me to be Christians?
Is it to give us a warm glow inside? Is it to make us happy
people? Is it solely to forgive us our sins? Listen to the
apostle Paul: 'He [God] chose us in him [Christ] before
the creation of the world to be holy and blameless in his
sight . . . Christ loved the church and gave himself up for
her to make her holy, cleansing her by the washing with
water through the word, and to present her to himself as
a radiant church, without stain or wrinkle or any other
blemish, but holy and blameless' (Ephesians 1:4; 5:25–27).
Holiness is the aim of our calling (election) and our salvation. It is God's fundamental requirement of us: 'It is
God's will that you should be sanctified . . . God did not
call us to be impure, but to live a holy life' (1 Thessalonians
4:3, 7). 'Just as he who called you is holy, so be holy in all

you do; for it is written: "Be holy, because I am holy" '
(1 Peter 1:15–16, quoting Leviticus 11:44–45).

The problem is that, as believers in today's world, we
are taken up with other priorities – albeit worthy ones. We
are very busy at our meetings, we are too busy sorting
ourselves out spiritually, and sorting others out spiritually,
to care too much about holiness. Read these words from
J. I. Packer: 'Though we routinely affirm the reality of
divine wrath against our sins, save as Christ's shed blood
covers them, we do not think much about God's revealed
hatred of sin in his own adopted family, nor do we "tremble
at his word" as our forebears did, fearful lest they offend
him (see Isaiah 66:2; Ezra 10:3), nor do we display that
abhorrence of ungodly things that Jude had in mind when
he spoke of "hating even the garment spotted by the flesh"
(Jude 23). It is our habit to think of the Father, the Son,
and the Holy Spirit as pally rather than pure, and to
dismiss as sub-Christian any idea that God's first concern
in his dealings with us might be to train us in righteousness
as a step toward future joy, rather than to load us with
present pleasures. We are not in tune with the biblical
perception of sin as pollution – *dirt*, to use a four-letter
word – in the eyes of God, and when we find Scripture
telling us that there are ways of behaving that God positively hates (see, for example, Psalms 5:4–6; 7:11–13; Proverbs 6:16; Isaiah 1:14; 61:8; Amos 5:21; Luke 16:15) we
treat it as imaginative exaggeration. No wonder, then, that
the quest for holiness among us has so largely petered out.'
(From *Keep In Step With the Spirit*. I gladly acknowledge
chapter 3 of that book as the basis of this section.)

The way of holiness

● Our union with Christ.
  □ When we become Christians, we have been moved
  over to God's side, we are 'separated' or 'set apart' (to
  use one of the meanings of the biblical word for *sanctify*)

for him. Our daily growing in holiness works out from
this basis. We will grow more like our God and our
Saviour as we continually give ourselves to him, turning
away daily from what God has shown us to be wrong in
our lives. We are to act out in life our God-given salvation, in an attitude of reverence and awe, because God
is active in our lives (Philippians 2:12–13). The more we
go on as believers, the more we will see the 'exceeding
sinfulness of sin' inside us – our motives, our emotions,
the spring from which our words, our pride, our sins
flow. The longer we live, the *greater* will be our dependence on Christ.

☐ We are united with Christ by the Spirit through faith.
We have been crucified and raised with Christ (Galatians 2:20). Romans 6 teaches us that we have been crucified with Christ: an end has been put to our lives that
were once dominated by sin. And more: we have been
raised with him to live a new life. In our inner beings
(Romans 7:22) 'self' has been removed from the throne
and we have been given a new heart (Ezekiel 36:26–27):
one that wants to respond to God and love him. So being
holy is becoming *in reality* what we *already are in principle*.
'Become what you are' is the essence of the call to holiness (Ephesians 5:8).

● The work of the Holy Spirit.
It is the Holy Spirit who brings about holiness. God is
at work *in* us (end of Romans 8:5; Philippians 2:13). The
Spirit does this chiefly by using what are known as
the 'means of grace' – reading the Bible and hearing it
preached, praying, worshipping, fellowship, sharing in
Holy Communion (Acts 2:42). It is as we open ourselves
up to such objective means that something subjective
goes on inside us: our motives are laid bare, our thoughts
are re-directed, our actions are questioned. In this way,
our *habits* are changed by the Holy Spirit (not us!): he
develops his fruit in us (Galatians 5:22–23).

- The fight within us.
  As Christians we aim each day to be like Christ, to love *him* utterly and to follow *him* completely. Yet we fail. Why? Because sin still lives in us. A battle is going on inside us: between the still surviving desires of the sinful nature within us and the tendencies of our new hearts, directed by the Spirit (Galatians 5:17). In our heart of hearts, all that we want to do is to please God. But still there is antagonism from the (sinful) world, the flesh (our sinful nature), and the devil. The good thing we really *want* to do is what we don't want to do. And we do the bad thing we don't want to do. We're like the person Paul describes in Romans 7:14–25. We constantly fall short of perfection. It is only by uncomfortably battling onwards, with prayer and God's help, that any progress is made. Our lives are like a building site: bad habits have to be demolished, and good Christian habits have to take their place. This is all carried out by Christ, through the Spirit, according to the plan of our Father architect. At the moment, our lives may look like a 'disaster area' with so many changes going on; yet one day all the construction work will result in something complete and beautiful (see Romans 7:24–25; Ephesians 5:25–27).

- The principles of law – and love.
  Our calling is to live up to God's law, his requirements of us. We don't do this to *earn* God's salvation; it is a working-out of our salvation. And we need to remember that God's requirements of us aren't a pharisaical code of practice that covers every tiny detail of our lives (including, for example, what we should wear to church, what food we should eat, how we should spend our leisure time). As Christians, we seek to keep the law in a non-legalistic way, out of a heart-devotion to our God – because we love him (Luke 7:47). This love is more than a feeling: it's a way of life, a commitment.

- Finally, two questions that bother some:

  □ Is sanctification a crisis or a process? The general teaching is that we gradually become more Christ-like (Romans 6:19; 2 Corinthians 3:18; Colossians 3:10). And there may well be certain times when the implications of our following Christ come home to us in an intense manner, making a sudden enormous impact on our lives.

  □ Are we passive or active in sanctification? Do we 'rest in Christ' or do we fight and strive? The New Testament has both emphases. We rest in Christ: we trust him; we give ourselves to him, we abide in him; *he* is our holiness (John 15:1–10; 1 Corinthians 1:30; Galatians 2:20). Yet also we are active, putting to death the old nature and putting on our new Christ-like nature. Notice that it is *we who do this*, and this action is *with the Spirit's help*. And notice too this is spelt out in detail, (Romans 8:13; 12:1–21; Galatians 5:13–26; Colossians 3:1–17).

> Holy Spirit, truth divine,
> Dawn upon this soul of mine;
> Word of God, and inward light,
> Wake my spirit, clear my sight.
>
> Holy Spirit, love divine,
> Glow within this heart of mine;
> Kindle every high desire;
> Perish self in Thy pure fire.
>
> Holy Spirit, power divine,
> Fill and nerve this will of mine;
> By Thee may I strongly live,
> Bravely bear, and nobly strive.
>
> Holy Spirit, right divine,
> King within my conscience reign;

Be my Lord, and I shall be
Firmly bound, for ever free.

Holy Spirit, peace divine,
Still this restless heart of mine;
Speak to calm this tossing sea,
Stayed in Thy tranquillity.

Holy Spirit, joy divine,
Gladden Thou this heart of mine;
In the desert ways I'll sing:
Spring, O Well, for ever spring!

Samuel Longfellow, 1819–92

Conclusion

Holy Christians are not those whose lives are aimed at holiness as such, but those whose lives are centred fully on the Lord Jesus Christ.

'Just as he who called you is holy, so be holy in all you do' (1 Peter 1:15).

5

GROWING IN FRUITFULNESS

> *Key thought* The Holy Spirit changes our characters.
> He wants to develop certain qualities in us.
>
> *Key Bible verse* 'The fruit of the Spirit is love, joy, peace,
> patience, kindness, goodness, faithfulness, gentleness
> and self-control. Against such things there is no law'
> (Galatians 5:22–23).

Our lifestyle

In the Gospels, human actions and speech are considered
to be fruit that grows from a person's inner being – see,
for example, Matthew 3:7–10. In Matthew 7 we see Jesus'
explanation to his disciples that people's true characters
are seen in their actions. 'Every good tree bears good fruit,
but a bad tree bears bad fruit. A good tree cannot bear
bad fruit, and a bad tree cannot bear good fruit' (Matthew
7:17–18). Our character is shown by what comes out of
us, particularly in our speech (Matthew 12:35–37).

The fruit of the Spirit: Galatians 5:22–23

In his letter to the Galatians, Paul contrasts the acts of the
sinful nature with the fruit of the Spirit. The acts of the
sinful nature are intense and violent, while the fruit of the
Spirit is gentle. 'It is a contrast like that between a drunken
orgy and the silent growth of spring flowers in the soil.
They belong to different worlds; the one so full of bluster,

noise and rowdy disturbance; the other quiet, meek, sweet
and patient' (William Still).

Notice that the nine 'fruits' are grouped under the singular *fruit*: all the characteristics belong together as a unity.
They are the result of the Spirit's work.

● Love, joy, and peace.

   □ In some ways it would be enough for Paul just to have
written *love*. He would then have said it all, since true
love really covers all the other qualities of this spiritual
fruit. But love, as the greatest Christian virtue comes
first, after all God is love (1 John 4:8).

   □ Joy isn't a 'mere feeling of physical well-being. It is a
spiritual joy that is not extinguished by the most adverse
circumstances' (Geoffrey Wilson). An example of joy in
dire straits is to be found in Acts 16:25. Doctor Luke
delights in the emphasis on joy (e.g. Luke 2:10; 10:21;
15:10; 24:52; Acts 5:41; 8:8, 39; 13:52.) See also, of
course, Philippians 4:4–9.

   □ The main thinking of peace here is the assurance of
peace with God in a sure and certain relationship
through faith in Christ (Romans 5:1; see also p. 49).

● Patience, kindness, and goodness.

   □ Patience follows naturally from peace. It speaks of
being able to withstand the wrong (and sometime not
wrong!) behaviour of others without flying off the handle.
In the face of annoyance, opposition and harm, the person with this quality of the Spirit will not become pas-
sionately angry.

   One of my favourite books is a book of games to do
while waiting – for the bus, for exam results, for that
letter to arrive or that phone call to come. In our 'instant'
age, waiting doesn't come easily. So the quality of patience is something the Spirit needs to cultivate in us.

   □ I confess I particularly like the word *kind*, as it seems
to be a beautifully active word, without any senti-
mentality attached to it. (I think of helping an old lady

across a street as an example of being kind, but obviously 'kind' means much more than this.) Yet God is kind even to the ungrateful (Luke 6:35). He *is* kind (Romans 2:4). And of course Christ is kind (e.g. Luke 8:40–56; 18:15–17). A mark of the Christian church is kindness (Ephesians 4:32).

☐ Goodness is the quality that benefits others. It is another aspect that finds practical and positive expression in our relationship with others. Goodness 'expects no rewards, and it stems from a heart of purity and openness. It points other people to God' (Richard Bewes).

- Faithfulness, gentleness, and self-control.
   ☐ Faithfulness is loyalty – to God, his word, and his gospel and to people. Such a faithfulness will withstand any deception or mockery. It is not suspicious, but gentle and strong.
   ☐ Gentleness isn't a weakness in which everyone crawls over you, using you as a door-mat. It's a strength that has been controlled, a true humility (Numbers 12:3; Matthew 11:29–30).
   ☐ Self-control is the means by which we keep ourselves – and the acts of the sinful nature – in check. Indeed, every thought is to be brought under Christ's mastery (2 Corinthians 10:5).

- 'Against such things there is no law.' As William Still helpfully comments: 'It takes all the heavenly activity in a man's soul to produce such gracious fruit. Is it because they are so modest that there is no law against them? Doubtless; but it is a vast understatement. The full truth is that these so fulfil the law of love as to transcend any formulation not expressed in terms of love and its gracious restraints and service. There are many unlawful "laws" against these fruits, because they madden evil men, but there is no law formulated that can accuse

them, as they soar far above legal or moral niceties in
the rich quality of their product.'

Keeping up with the Spirit

How can we see such fruit grow in our lives, remembering
that such fruit isn't first and foremost to be eaten ourselves
or to be admired as an attractive display. The fruit is
there for our starving world – a world starved of love, joy,
peace . . .

The context of the verses in Galatians 5:22–23 shows us
the way: by keeping in step with the Holy Spirit. As we
keep up with him, our hearts submitted to his control, so
we will make progress. The Spirit as the controller of our
lives will direct us, and we will move onwards. We are 'not
to run ahead and not to lag behind. This involves the
Word, prayer, worship, praise, and fellowship with God's
people. It also means "pulling out the weeds" so that the
seed of the Word can take root and bear fruit' (Warren W.
Wiersbe). All this is a helpful commentary on the famous
passage in John 15:1–8. Jesus is the vine and the Father is
the gardener. As believers, we are carefully looked after by
our gardener, who takes care to prune us so that we might
be even more fruitful (verse 2). This fruitfulness is only
possible if we remain in him and his words in us (verses
4–7). Our fruitfulness has its roots in Jesus himself and it
is up to us to stay intimately close to him (verse 4). The
sap, the source of our fruit-bearing, comes from the one to
whom we are vitally connected by his Spirit, our Lord
Jesus Christ.

Take time to be holy, speak oft with thy Lord;
Abide in Him always, and feed on His Word.
Make friends of God's children, help those who are weak;
Forgetting in nothing His blessing to seek.

Take time to be holy, the world rushes on;

Spend much time in secret with Jesus alone.
By looking to Jesus like Him thou shalt be;
Thy friends, in thy conduct, His likeness shall see.

Take time to be holy, let Him be thy guide:
And run not before Him whatever betide:
In joy or in sorrow still follow thy Lord,
And, looking to Jesus, still trust in His Word.

Take time to be holy, be calm in thy soul;
Each thought and each temper beneath His control.
Thus led by His Spirit and filled with His love,
Thou soon shalt be fitted for service above.

William Dunn Longstaff, 1822–94

Conclusion

To show the fruit of the Spirit means quite simply to be like Christ.

'I am the vine; you are the branches. If a man remains in me and I in him, he will bear much fruit; apart from me you can do nothing' (Jesus, in John 15:4–5).

6

GROWING IN POWER

> *Key thought* The Holy Spirit wants to give the church
> his power so that our lives can be holy and effective
> for God.
>
> *Key Bible verse* 'You will receive power when the Holy
> Spirit comes on you; and you will be my witnesses in
> Jerusalem, and in all Judea and Samaria, and to the
> ends of the earth' (Jesus, in Acts 1:8).

'You will receive power'

These were the closing words of Jesus before he was taken
up into heaven (Acts 1:8).

Jim Packer describes power as 'the sense of God-given
ability to do what you know you ought to do and indeed
want to do, but feel that you lack the strength for'. Power
is a dominant theme in the Acts of the Apostles. The Holy
Spirit in Acts:

- brings power for witnessing (1:8; 4:29–33) and serving
  (6:3–5).

- works when God's people are united and pray together
  (2:2, 42–47; 4:31).

- guides individual Christians (8:29; 16:7) and churches
  (13:2).

- gives miraculous gifts, for example speaking in other
  languages (2:4), prophecy (11:28), and miracles (14:3).

In fact it is not really the apostles who initiate the evangelism in Acts, it is the Holy Spirit (hence, the Bible book is sometimes referred to as 'the Acts of the Holy Spirit').

- first inspires Peter to preach the gospel in Jerusalem (chapter 2).

- guides Stephen, as Michael Green puts it, to 'break out of the narrow confines of law-keeping and temple worship' to reach the Grecian Jews (6:3, 5).

- brings those who were 'beyond the pale', spiritually speaking, into the church: those from Samaria (8:14), the Ethiopian eunuch (8:26–40), the Gentiles such as the God-fearing Cornelius (chapter 10) and those in other towns (e.g. Lystra, 14:8–19).

Supernatural power

We cannot deny or run away from this power! It's evident in the Old Testament, in the Gospels, Acts, and in the New Testament letters. The power of the Spirit of God is seen in the resurrection of Jesus (Romans 8:11). And it is this power that is at work for us as believers (Ephesians 1:19–20) and is a vital part of our inner resources (Ephesians 3:16–21; Philippians 3:10).

Paul prays for the Romans that they 'may overflow with hope by the power of the Holy Spirit' (15:13). What Christ has done through him, he goes on, is 'by the power of signs and miracles, through the power of the Spirit' (15:18–19). The gospel of Jesus Christ crucified that he preached at Corinth was undertaken 'with a demonstration of the Spirit's power, so that your faith might . . . rest on . . . God's power' (1 Corinthians 2:4–5). Writing about his 'thorn in the flesh', Paul states that the Lord said to him, 'My grace is sufficient for you, for my power is made perfect in weakness.' 'Therefore,' said Paul, 'I will boast all the more gladly about my weaknesses, so that Christ's power may rest on me' (2 Corinthians 12:9). Jim Packer's conclusion from these and other verses is 'What we are being told is that supernatural living through supernatural empowering is at the very heart of New Testament Christianity, so that those who, while professing faith, do not experience and show forth this empowering are suspect by New Testament standards' (*Keep in Step with the Spirit*).

Power and us . . . and how?

Let's stop and be honest with ourselves. Don't we need power to tell others about Jesus? I find it difficult to talk about Jesus. I need the Spirit's power (the power of Jesus). I need God's help (= his power) to love other people genuinely. I need his power to live as a believer, to do my work, to be the husband and father, to be the church member that God wants me to be. And I imagine that it's similar for you. You see, often we know *what* to do, but we lack the power to do it. We may go to conference after conference or meeting after meeting where we hear new methods to follow, yet we still lack the power to put these into practice. (I over-generalize, but I think you know what I mean.)

We can't escape our responsibilities (much as we'd like to sometimes). Do you remember that passage in the Gospels where Jesus, talking about the coming of the Spirit, says that he (the Spirit) will testify about him (Jesus). Then Jesus adds: 'And you also must testify' (John 15:26–27). Perhaps we can imagine the disciples thinking at first, 'Phew! We're let off the hook! The Holy Spirit will do it all!' No! We're to be involved, too!

How, then, does this power come to be ours? The following steps may be helpful.

- We need to see our need of God. Not just on the big occasions, but constantly. (Remember, 'be filled with the Spirit' is something ongoing, not a one-off experience.)

- We need to seek God.

  □ '*Ask* him' (i.e. God) is one of the phrases used to describe what we are to do to receive the Holy Spirit (Luke 11:13; the parallel verse, Matthew 7:11, has 'good gifts'. As Martyn Lloyd-Jones writes, 'in giving the Holy Spirit, He gives us everything; every fitness we require, every grace, every gift.')

  □ '*Thirst*' for him is another one of the words used (Matthew 5:6). Are you and I hungering and thirsting for *God*? Are we yearning for his righteousness? Or are we in it just for an exciting experience? This highlights our motives: how serious are you and I with God? Do we 'want power' so that others can say, 'There goes a Spirit-filled believer' or just so that others notice *our* power as we serve God and our fellow humans. Whose power is it anyway? Listen to the apostle Paul: 'We have this treasure in jars of clay [i.e. in us as weak finite creatures] to show that this all-surpassing power is from God and not from us' (2 Corinthians 4:7). The following verses should be read, too, because they show the suffering that came to Paul, and could well come our way in some shape or form when we're real with God (see also Philippians 3:10).

- Under the searchlight of God and his holiness, as we see our constant need of him, so God will point out to us things in our lives that need to be put right. We may have a big row with someone as our pride rears its ugly head once more. Or it may be that our motives need to get sorted out again. To use the biblical word, we need to *obey* God – to act according to his will – be it by doing something that we're neglecting to do, or by stopping something that we shouldn't be doing. Knowledge of God's will of course comes about by having God's input – the Bible – regularly in our lives. (Remember, the word of God is the 'sword of the Spirit', Ephesians 6:17.) Ideally we should read our Bibles daily, but since we don't live in an ideal world, let's at least *aim* at a daily meditation of God's word, and do our best to reach this aim. But then let's not allow the devil to get the upper hand with us by overwhelming us with a deep sense of guilt when we miss out on reading the Bible.

- It can be helpful to share our inner life with others – not in a large group, but with maybe just one other person whom we know and trust (or are beginning to). I've certainly known that such times of sharing together in seeking God honestly have been beneficial (Proverbs 27:17; Malachi 3:16).

- Is there another step? Yes – live it out! Live out the God-given life within you. You'll still stumble and fall spiritually. You'll learn gradually. You'll still need to come back to God saying you've got it wrong, you'll still need to seek God to clean up your motives. But live it out with the courage that he gives you! It may well be others who notice your growing Christlikeness, the difference in the way you live. Get involved in your church – or more particularly, with people. I confess I can't understand Christians who claim to have the power but seem to do nothing in a world of desperate need. They remind me of a rocket that is ready for lift-off but which stays on the launch-pad! If there really is power within us, then surely it will naturally show in some active service that is performed with a God-given confidence.

> Spirit of the living God, fall afresh on me
> Spirit of the living God, fall afresh on me
> Break me, melt me, mould me, fill me;
> Spirit of the living God, fall afresh on me.

Conclusion

Our word *dynamite* comes from one of the New Testament words for the power that the Holy Spirit gives us. His power is explosive! Sometimes this will be seen in spectacular ways, while often it will be seen in ways that are much more ordinary. But there will be a radical difference in the way we live.

'We have this treasure in jars of clay to show that this all-surpassing power is from God and not from us' (2 Corinthians 4:7).

7

GROWING IN REALITY

> *Key thought* The Holy Spirit wants to keep us in a fresh, living, vital relationship with Jesus so that we can serve our Saviour in the world today.
>
> *Key Bible verse* 'We, who with unveiled faces all reflect the Lord's glory, are being transformed into his likeness with ever-increasing glory, which comes from the Lord, who is the Spirit' (2 Corinthians 3:18).

Growing in reality

The Holy Spirit wants to make God real to the world today. And he wants to do this especially through believers. This happens as we grow in our lives with God: as we come to know God more, through Jesus Christ, by the Spirit. We experience God in a deeper way, we grow more like Christ. This is a lifelong process (2 Corinthians 3:18). In this section, let us look at some of the New Testament commands concerning the Holy Spirit.

- Do not resist the Holy Spirit.

  The possibility of resisting the Holy Spirit comes in Acts 7:51. Stephen has described God's plan through history. At the end of his speech he is blunt: 'You stiff-necked people, with uncircumcised hearts and ears! You are just like your fathers: You always resist the Holy Spirit!'

  Resisting the Holy Spirit means remaining blind and opposed to his purposes. The Holy Spirit wants to invade our lives. To resist him is to turn a deaf ear to his claims on our lives. As the apostle Paul wrote, 'Examine yourselves to see whether you are in the faith; test yourselves' (2 Corinthians 13:5). This is a solemn warning to all of us.

- Do not grieve the Holy Spirit.
  It is possible for believers to cause sorrow to the Holy Spirit, to grieve him. This word *grieve* occurs in Ephesians 4:30: the context is that of being sealed with the Holy Spirit for the day of redemption (see also Ephesians 1:13) and the behaviour of our lives as believers (see Ephesians 4:17—5:21). As G. Campbell Morgan comments, 'Whenever He is thwarted, whenever He is disobeyed, whenever He gives some new revelation of the Christ which brings no response, He is grieved. The heart of God is sad when, by the disobedience of His children, His purpose of grace in them is hindered. Alas! how often has the Holy Spirit been grieved; how often has He brought some vision of the Master that has made demands upon devotion, that has claimed new consecration; and because the way of devotion and the way of consecration are always the way of the Altar and the Cross, the children of His love have drawn back. The Spirit has been grieved, because hindered in His purposes; the day of the saints' perfecting has been postponed, and the coming of the kingdom of God has been delayed' (*The Spirit of God*).

- Do not put out the Spirit's fire.
  Putting out the Spirit's fire (1 Thessalonians 5:19; older versions had '(do not) *quench* the Spirit') refers to the vital activity of the Spirit in our service for God. The context is the treatment of prophecies and Paul advises his (newly-converted) readers to test what they hear, to hold on to the good, and to get rid of the evil (1 Thessalonians 5:19–22). We would do well to follow his advice, not rejecting every supernatural evidence of the Holy Spirit's work, but seeing if it is of God, and, if so, keeping

it. And of course if it is not of God, then it needs to be rejected.

● Keep in step with the Spirit.

To turn to some of the positive commands, this command comes in Galatians 5:25. We're reminded in the preceding verses of the need to grow, to allow the Spirit's fruit to develop in our lives (Galatians 5:22–23). These verses also show us that the Holy Spirit waits to move us on, in our lives individually, and as churches. Are you and I growing as believers? Is the church that you're a part of moving on? Or is it stuck in a time-warp of a hundred years ago – or three hundred years ago, or thirty years ago or even three years ago? I'm not thinking so much of a small group within a church 'zooming off into a higher, more rarified, more spiritual realm'. I'm thinking of a whole church, as a people bound together by the Spirit (Ephesians 4:3), moving on with God.

● Be aglow with the Spirit.

The NIV for this verse (Romans 12:11) has 'Keep your spiritual fervour'. Paul does not want his readers to be lacking in enthusiasm, but to be set on fire by the Spirit! The context of these verses is significant: warm, lowly, humble service (Romans 12:9–13)!

The fellowship of the Holy Spirit

Have you ever thought about the 'fellowship of the Holy Spirit'? Is it just the final third of 'the grace' that is spoken at the end of a meeting? No! It's a reference to his sharing in the work of the gospel today. William Hendriksen calls this fellowship 'the gift of the Spirit', '*grace* being the gift of the Lord Jesus Christ, *love* the gift of the Father'. I sometimes think of it this way: we need *grace* to deal with our sin. It is by grace that we are saved. This grace is seen in the death of our Lord Jesus Christ. And it springs from the love of God, our Father: the one who gave his only-begotten Son for us. But how do I now come to know Jesus' grace and the Father's love? Only by the helping work of the Holy Spirit: he is the one who makes these real in my life. He does this to me and to the 'all' of us in the prayer at the end of 2 Corinthians by his fellowship (see also Philippians 2:1). As Jim Packer says, 'Were it not for the work of the Holy Spirit there would be no gospel, no faith, no church, no Christianity in the world at all.' We'd be utterly lost without him: but in him and his fellowship all believers are united in Christ.

Revive us, Lord!

Don't you and I sense we need constantly to know the Spirit breaking into our lives in a fresh way? Don't we need a deeper moment-by-moment awareness of God, through Jesus, by the Spirit? How we need God to keep us in a real, living experience of himself! At times of revival – when God chooses to come down amongst his people in a special way – believers have a heightened sense of God and the power of his word, and therefore their own nothingness before him. May we pray for and seek such times when God chooses to revitalize his people.

> O Breath of Life, come sweeping through us,
>   Revive Thy church with life and power,
> O Breath of Life, come, cleanse, renew us,
>   And fit Thy church to meet this hour.
>
> O Wind of God, come, bend us, break us,
>   Till humbly we confess our need;
> Then in Thy tenderness remake us,
>   Revive, restore; for this we plead.
>
> O Breath of Love, come, breathe within us,
>   Renewing thought and will and heart:
> Come, Love of Christ, afresh to win us,
>   Revive Thy church in every part.

Revive us, Lord! Is zeal abating
   While harvest fields are vast and white?
Revive us, Lord, the world is waiting,
   Equip Thy church to spread the light.

Elizabeth Ann Head, 1850–1936

Conclusion

As individuals and as churches we need to stop and think about how much we are honouring the Holy Spirit.

'May the . . . fellowship of the Holy Spirit be with you all' (2 Corinthians 13:14).

8

WORKING IT OUT

Life in the Spirit

Where do our studies above the person and activity of the
Holy Spirit take us? We're led to:

- *a deeper reality in our worship of God.* To worship God is to
  respond to him. We enjoy fellowship with the Father
  and the Son, through the Spirit. In particular, Spirit-led
  worship will mean:

  □ focusing on the Lord Jesus Christ. To emphasize the
  work of the Holy Spirit means uplifting *Jesus* as the head
  of the body.

  □ a heart-response to God, prompted by the Spirit
  (Galatians 4:6).

  □ communication of the Bible: the Scriptures need to be
  explained and applied to us. This is the work of the
  Spirit, even as we undertake it. This won't mean that
  the absolutes of the Bible will be watered down; they
  remain non-negotiable. But it will mean, indeed it must
  mean, the application of the timeless biblical principles
  to the contemporary world. The Spirit 'always works in
  conjunction with the Word and hence our experience of
  the Spirit needs the continual check, balance and
  direction of the whole written Word of God' (Bruce
  Milne).

  □ a continuing hunger for more of God. We will cry
  with the psalmist: 'How lovely is your dwelling-place, O
  LORD Almighty! My soul yearns, even faints, for the
  courts of the LORD; my heart and my flesh cry out for
  the living God' (Psalm 84:1–2).

● *a greater love for others.* If the Spirit is truly working in us then he will instil in us a sense of responsibility for the world. A biblical mark of the work of the Spirit is not so much a desire to see the spectacular, as to be involved in evangelism and mission (Acts 1:8). And the best way we can love the world is to evangelize it. Said Jesus: 'Whoever believes in me . . . streams of living water will flow from within him.' And John adds: 'By this he meant the Spirit . . .' (John 7:37–39). Isn't the spiritually parched world around us crying out desperately for living water? Are we responding to that cry?

● *a fuller experience of our own humanity.* As we know the working of the Spirit in our lives, so we will become more and more fully human. In other words, as we become more dependent on God, we will know increasingly what it means to be a man or woman of God. Again, as we, with the Spirit's help, love others in Jesus' name so we will find ourselves becoming the people God intended us to be. We will become more like Jesus in our character, not because of our own efforts, but because the Spirit is giving new life within us. We will experience difficulties and trouble, to be sure, yet there will still be the Spirit of simple joy within us. We will also know what it means to share with others in the new life God has called us to. 'The Spirit who unites us to Christ unites us in that act to all God's people; our sanctification through the Spirit's renewing influence is set firmly in the context of the fellowship of God's people, particularly in the local church to which he calls us. The Spirit knows nothing of one-man-band Christians and ministries. We need to beware of claims to the Spirit's leading which have no explicit "check" at the corporate level. Rather, among the most enriching dimensions of his work are those relationships of love and sharing which he gives us within the life of the family of God' (Bruce Milne, *Know the Truth*).

' "If anyone is thirsty, let him come to me and drink. Whoever believes in me, as the Scripture has said, streams of living water will flow from within him." By this he meant the Spirit, whom those who believed in him were later to receive' (Jesus, in John 7:37–39).

Belonging to the church

1

THE PROMISE OF THE
CHURCH

Key thought One of the deepest human needs is to know
that we belong. As Christians we belong to the family
of God, his church.

Key Bible verse 'God placed all things under his feet
and appointed him to be head over everything for the
church, which is his body, the fulness of him who fills
everything in every way' (Ephesians 1:22–23).

What is the church?

The word 'church' is used in two main ways in the Bible:
- All those who believe in the Lord Jesus Christ: all, living
  or dead, who have been saved by him. This is sometimes
  known as the 'church universal' (Matthew 16:18; Ephesians 1:22; 3:10, 21; 5:23–32).
- A group of believers in a particular area (Matthew 18:17;
  1 Corinthians 1:2; 11:16; 14:19).

The called ones

The word for church in Greek is *ekklesia*. (We get our word
'ecclesiastical' from this.) The word *ekklesia* is used to refer
to a group of people who met together, an assembly (Acts
19:32, 39, 41). The word also has a Hebrew background;
in the Greek version of the Old Testament it is a translation
of the Hebrew *qahal*. Together the two word groups occur
more than 700 times in the Old and New Testaments. To
take this further, we can say that the people of God are:

- *called out* – as Israel was from Egypt (Hosea 11:1). Similarly, Christians are called out or delivered from sin and
death. Who does the calling? God does! This speaks of
his sovereignty, his choosing, his power, his authority.
It puts our efforts in the right perspective. It is his
activity that counts ultimately; 'we can never be more
than his servants who seek to obey their Master as they
work within his church' (David Watson).

- *called for* – a relationship with God. This is the expression
of God's covenant, his firm agreement of friendship (see
pp. 8–11) with his people. So we're not a club with dos
and don'ts but a group of people who have a living
relationship with our God.

- *called together* – to make up a new community. We're not
just called individually, but together. Being a Christian
is more than something private, personal, just involving
'me and Jesus'. It's something we do together – or better,
something we *are* together. This reminds us that the
depth of the relationship between the members of a
church is more important than the number of activities
we're involved in.

- *called to* – a future inheritance. Israel was called to the
promised land (Canaan); for Christians the destination
at the end of our journey is heaven. Have you and I, I
wonder, lost something of a sense of going somewhere?
We're to be a people on the move for God!

The church of the living God

How did the church come into being?

- Through the Father's sovereign action in grace, He chose a people for himself, redeemed by the blood of his Son (Ephesians 1:4–14).

- The true foundation of the church is Christ (1 Corinthians 3:11). The apostles are, in a secondary sense, the foundation (Matthew 16:17–18; Ephesians 2:20).

- The church was brought into being by the death of Christ (Acts 20:28). His resurrection proves that the sacrifice of himself was sufficient for our sin; the coming of his Spirit following his ascension marks the church's 'birthday' (Acts 2).

Here are some of the promises for all those who have been saved and born again and so are part of the church of the living God. The church:

- was promised by the Lord Jesus Christ (Matthew 16:18);
- was promised Christ as its head (Ephesians 1:22; 4:15; 5:23);
- exists to make known the wisdom of God (Ephesians 3:10);
- shows the glory of God (Ephesians 3:21);
- can claim promises to be fulfilled in the work of disciple-making (Matthew 28:19–20);
- can lay hold of promised gifts (Ephesians 4:4–13);
- has been given fulness in Christ (Colossians 2:10);
- has Christ as its promised cornerstone (Ephesians 2:20; 1 Peter 2:6);
- has Christ's promised love (Ephesians 5:25);
- has Christ's promised care (Ephesians 5:29; 1 Peter 5:7);
- has Christ's promised protection and preservation (Matthew 16:18; John 10:28);
- has Christ's promised presence (Matthew 18:20; John 14:16; Hebrews 13:5);

- has the promise of additions to its numbers (Acts 1:8; 2:47);
- has a God-given spiritual unity (John 17:21–22; 1 Corinthians 10:17; 12:12–31; Galatians 3:28; Ephesians 4:3–4);
- is promised union and communion with Christ (John 17:24; Ephesians 2:13, 18; Hebrews 12:22, 24);
- is promised a glorious future (John 14:3; Ephesians 5:27; Revelation 21:1–4).

Work at it!

Does your heart leap as you read of these marvellous promises? Mine does! I'm reminded that 'church' isn't an 'add-on' in my life, just a building where I spend Sundays, or an activity in which I'm involved on weekday nights. I'm reminded that the church is a living, dynamic expression of God's activity in the world of today. I'm reminded that the church is about people – and supremely about God.

Does this fire my involvement when I get discouraged at the apparent lack of progress in the tasks God has given me? Yes! I'm about the king's business! Does it humble me when I think of the church as merely a human institution? Yes! I'm reminded that *Jesus* is building *his* church. I'm re-energized with a God-given confidence to be a partner with Jesus in his work.

> The church's one foundation
>   Is Jesus Christ her Lord;
> She is His new creation
>   By water and the Word;
> From heaven He came and sought her
>   To be His holy bride;
> With His own blood He bought her,
>   And for her life He died.

Elect from every nation,
   Yet one o'er all the earth;
Her charter of salvation –
   One Lord, one faith, one birth;
One holy Name she blesses,
   Partakes one holy food;
And to one hope she presses,
   With every grace endued.

Though with a scornful wonder
   Men see her sore oppressed,
By schisms rent asunder,
   By heresies distressed,
Yet saints their watch are keeping,
   Their cry goes up, 'How long?'
And soon the night of weeping
   Shall be the morn of song.

'Mid toil and tribulation,
   And tumult of her war,
She waits the consummation
   Of peace for evermore;
Till with the vision glorious
   Her longing eyes are blest,
And the great church victorious
   Shall be the church at rest.

Yet she on earth hath union
   With God the Three in One,
And mystic sweet communion
   With those whose rest is won.
O happy ones and holy!
   Lord, give us grace that we,
Like them, the meek and lowly,
   On high may dwell with Thee!

Samuel John Stone, 1839–1900

Conclusion

The church of Christ is the group of all saved people. It is *his* church: *he* is active, to fulfil *his* purposes.

'I will build my church, and the gates of Hades [or hell] will not overcome it' (Jesus, in Matthew 16:18).

2

GOD'S PLAN FOR THE CHURCH

Key thought There are several different pictures of the church in the New Testament. Looking at them, we see what is God's plan for the church and what our part is to be.

Key Bible verse 'But you are a chosen people, a royal priesthood, a holy nation, a people belonging to God, that you may declare the praises of him who called you out of darkness into his wonderful light. Once you were not a people, but now you are the people of God; once you had not received mercy, but now you have received mercy' (1 Peter 2:9–10).

Get involved!

We saw in the last section that the word 'church' is used in two main ways – to speak of all those who throughout history are believers ('the church universal') and a smaller microcosm of this: a local group of believers. To be more precise, in the New Testament those who became Christians were immediately baptized and became part of a local church (Acts 2:37–41; 9:18–19, 26; 18:1–11). In other words, the New Testament knows nothing of the solitary, 'go-it-alone' Christian. To check this out, you could get hold of a concordance and see how many times the words 'saint' (singular) and 'saints' (plural) occur in the New Testament. In the Authorized Version, there are sixty -one occurrences of 'saints' (plural) and only one of the singular

– and that's 'Salute [greet] every saint in Christ Jesus' (Philippians 4:21). In the New International Version, all are in the plural! So we see that 'the concept of a solitary saint is foreign to the New Testament writers' (Michael Griffiths, *Cinderella with Amnesia*). At conversion, Christians identified themselves with a particular local church – that's where they got stuck in.

Let me be personal. Have you done this? Are you involved with a local group of believers? Or are you bemoaning the fact that there's nowhere in your area that's 'up to scratch'? No church is perfect, of course – if it was, as soon as you or I joined it, we'd make it imperfect! This troubled me a few years ago – then I suddenly thought about Paul's letters: he wrote them to imperfect churches, to guide them on their way. They needed teaching, encouragement, advice, instructing, warning. Why? Just because they were imperfect! So do we – we need God's imput into our lives in a local church to make us become the people God intended us to be.

One further personal reminder. Back to Michael Griffiths again: I was once at a meeting where he asked all of us to make up a sentence about 'the church'. You could do well to follow his suggestion. Have you thought of one? Now – what does your sentence begin with: *they* ('*They* do this at the church I go to'), or *it* ('*It's* very dull')? To be fully biblical, our sentence should begin with *we* ('*We* do this . . .'). Do you see? Do we think of the church as a group of people that we don't feel part of (*they*) or as a thing (*it*)? Or do we think of the church as a group of people that *we* are committed to and as a people we're involved with? (You listen to some of your friends and see what they say as well!)

So much for these two preliminary points, then: that God's plan is that we should not exist just as individual solitary believers; and the importance of the word 'we', the real identifying with and involvement in a local church. These two points are vital because if they aren't part of us, then discussion of some of the pictures of the church is abstract and unrelated to our own experience.

Do you get the picture?

Here, then, are some of the picture-descriptions, the 'visual aids' of the church in the New Testament. The church is

- *a family or household*. We are members of God's household (Ephesians 2:19; 1 Timothy 3:15), part of his family (Ephesians 3:14–15). This reminds us again of being together. No one is to be a stranger, all are to be integrated as children are in a family. 'This is what the congregation ought to mean to us – a place where we feel safe, can be ourselves, and have no need to be boarded up behind a façade, a place where we are cared for and care for one another' (Michael Griffiths). The church is meant to be somewhere where we can relax (rather than have to get dressed up for in formal clothes!). It's good that the church is re-discovering today the importance of using our homes (Acts 20:20). Often we can relax more in the physical environment of a home – so house-groups in a church can be important.

- *a body*. We are all different parts of a body, with Christ as its head (1 Corinthians 12:12–31). This shows us that the church is made up of different parts, just as our bodies are. It also shows us that all are important. A friend recently broke her little toe. Not only was it very painful, it also made her far less mobile! Even when something small is out of joint, the whole body cannot function properly. So no member of the body can be thought to be unimportant. The opposite is also true: no member of the body is more important than all the others. I once asked a group of young people what they thought the most important jobs in the church were. 'Preaching,' said some. 'Teaching,' others. No – the answer is: all the tasks are important! Just think of the

average church service: at the end we thank the preacher
– but someone else put the chairs out, someone else
swept the floor, someone else checked the heating; if
there was a visiting speaker, someone wrote to them
months before, and so on. Do they get thanked? All are
important; we all need each other, and, supremely, we
all depend upon Christ, our head. We are to carry out
his instructions.

Notice, too, in Ephesians 4:11–13 the task of the
church leaders (verse 11) is to get the people in a fit (or
prepared or equipped) state to do works of service (verse
12). The leaders aren't to do it all! Their task is to train
others to do things. The result? The building up of the
church, unity, and maturity (end of verse 12, and verse
13).

● *a building.* We are part of a spiritual building, made up
of 'living stones' (1 Peter 2:4–5). The 'building' is still
under construction (1 Corinthians 3:9–13). This shows
again how all are necessary – one stone missing means
a gap, all the stones together result in strength – and
how we depend on each other, and above all, on Christ,
the cornerstone (Ephesians 2:20; 1 Peter 2:6). This building isn't made up of bricks and mortar but a spiritual
sacrifice of praise (Hebrews 13:15).

The church, then, is the people of God – chosen by
him. We are 'a royal priesthood, a holy nation, a people
belonging to God'. Our purpose is that we 'may declare
the praises of him who called us out of darkness into his
wonderful light' (1 Peter 2:9–10).

● *a bride.* This is surely the most beautiful picture of the
church (Ephesians 5:25–27). We see something deeply
intimate when we think that the church is to be 'married'
to Christ. The goal of the church is to become beautiful,
God's perfect new society, 'without stain or wrinkle or
any other blemish, but holy and blameless' (Ephesians
5:27) – perfect in holiness, pure in teaching (2 Corinthi-

ans 11:2–4). The apostle John had a vision of the church 'prepared as a bride beautifully dressed for her husband' (Revelation 21:2). We already enjoy an intimate union with God and we are to prepare ourselves for that day in the future when the bride will meet her husband (Revelation 21:9). On that day, as the hymn puts it,

> The bride eyes not her garment,
>   But her dear bridegroom's face;
> I will not gaze at glory,
>   But on my King of grace;
> Not at the crown He giveth,
>   But on His piercèd hand:
> The Lamb is all the glory
>   Of Immanuel's land.

*

> Church of God, elect and glorious,
>   holy nation, chosen race;
> called as God's own special people,
>   royal priests and heirs of grace:
> know the purpose of your calling,
>   show to all his mighty deeds;
> tell of love which knows no limits,
>   grace which meets all human needs.

> God has called you out of darkness
>   into his most marvellous light;
> brought his truth to life within you,
>   turned your blindness into sight:
> let your light so shine around you
>   that God's name is glorified;
> and all find fresh hope and purpose
>   in Christ Jesus crucified.

> Once you were an alien people,
>   strangers to God's heart of love,
> but he brought you home in mercy,
>   citizens of heaven above:

let his love flow out to others,
    let them feel a Father's care;
that they too may know his welcome,
    and his countless blessings share.

Church of God, elect and holy,
    be the people he intends;
strong in faith and swift to answer
    each command your master sends:
royal priests, fulfil your calling
    through your sacrifice and prayer;
give your lives in joyful service –
    sing his praise, his love declare.

                                      James Seddon, 1915–1983

Conclusion
The church is a living fellowship, not an organization
or a building; a close family, rather than a group of
individuals. Our task now is to become the people he
intends. One day the church as the bride of Christ
will come to full and perfect beauty for her wedding
with the Lamb.

'Christ loved the church and gave himself up for her
to make her holy . . . to present her to himself as a
radiant church, without stain or wrinkle or any other
blemish, but holy and blameless' (Ephesians 5:25–27).

THE MARKS OF A CHURCH

Key thought Certain guidelines stand out in the life of one church in the New Testament. If we're courageous enough to work them out ourselves, God will surely lead us into good things, for his glory.

Key Bible verse 'Those who had been scattered by the persecution in connection with Stephen travelled as far as Phoenicia, Cyprus and Antioch, telling the message only to Jews. Some of them, however, men from Cyprus and Cyrene, went to Antioch and began to speak to Greeks also, telling them the good news about the Lord Jesus. The Lord's hand was with them, and a great number of people believed and turned to the Lord' (Acts 11:19–21).

Antioch: population 300,000, the third largest city in the Roman Empire of the first century. What was the church in Antioch like? The church there grew by people becoming converted (Acts 11:21, 24). You could see that the Christians were different people – because of the work of God in their lives (Acts 11:23). The Christians weren't inward-looking. God spoke to them and they responded positively (Acts 11:28–30; 13:2–3). What, then, were some of the secrets of their 'success'?

Everyone was involved

Look at Acts 11:19–20. The 'ordinary' Christians had been scattered by persecution. What did they do? Clam up? No!

They got involved naturally in the task of sharing the gospel in an everyday way (verse 20). There was no big name – even Barnabas didn't come till later (verse 22)! They shared the gospel by speaking to people and telling them the good news about the Lord Jesus. How about us? Do we think it is enough only to live an upright life and never tell anyone about Jesus? Or do we just invite people to services without telling them the good news ourselves?

They broke new ground

Acts 11:20 also shows us that the Christians in Antioch took the initiative. Up to this time, the Christians had been speaking to the Jews or those with links with the Jewish community (e.g. Acts 2:5; 10:2, 22). Now, however, men from Cyprus and Cyrene did something new: they began to talk to Gentile Greeks who had no Jewish links. As John Benton writes ('Seven secrets of a successful church', *Evangelical Times*): 'This was "Christian" innovation. Their new move was not a gimmick, but came out of the constraint of Christian love. These Christians, who had lived among the Gentiles, were moved with concern for their eternal future and felt they must speak. Furthermore, they rightly understood the prophecies concerning Christ being a light to the Gentiles, which some had misinterpreted; and so they could, if asked, give some scriptural reasons for their action.

'They were not afraid to do something new. They were not always looking over their shoulder and asking: "Is this the way the top brass in Jerusalem do things?" They were prepared to think for themselves from Scripture about such questions as: does this approach truly glorify Christ? Does this method honestly sow the word? Does it make the gospel clear? If so, let's do it!'

How about us? Are we breaking fresh ground in our methods of presenting the gospel in our present generation?

The leadership was realistic and shared

Every church needs leadership (Acts 14:23; Ephesians
4:11–12); the leadership in Antioch was realistic. Barnabas,
'Mr Encouragement', quickly set up a nurture group to
look after new believers (Acts 11:23). His presence there
seems also to have spurred on further evangelism and reap-
ing (Acts 11:24). But Barnabas was also aware of his own
limitations – so he sent for Paul (Acts 11:25).

As leaders we can, I guess, want to hang on to our own
work (and build our own little empires, to put it unkindly).
A shared leadership, however, although painful at times,
can be much more effective. Look at the variety of leaders
mentioned in Acts 13:1 – and they were prophets and
teachers. As Michael Green (*Evangelism – now and then*) puts
it, 'Now it would be hard to find more uncomfortable
bedfellows than that. The prophet is always tending to
move on instinct; you never know what the man is going
to do next. And the teacher is painfully predictable. To
use contemporary language, the prophet is "charismatic"
and the teacher is not. This is one of the hottest issues in
a number of churches of all denominations all over the
world at the moment. Antioch solved it by having both
types represented in the leadership. How wise they were!
This meant that the worship combined the warm spiritu-
ality of the charismatics and the balanced teaching ministry
of the teachers. How rarely is that balance found in a
modern church, but what a power it is when the combination comes off. It is tragic to me when "charismatic"
Christians write off as second-class Christians the men who
could so deepen their understanding of the faith; and when
"non-charismatics" fear what the "charismatics" bring –
the very elements of life, expectancy, and vibrant sense of
the reality of God which most churches could do with.
There was no such divide at Antioch. Nor need there be
in our own day.'

Their worship was dynamic

● *Their teaching was centred on Christ* (Acts 11:26). The over-riding passion of the church was Christ – so much so that they were given the name 'Christian'.

● *They were serious in their worship* (it included fasting). They were real. They were united. Look at their church meeting (Acts 13:1–2). They were sensitive to God and, no doubt, to each other. You can almost sense the 'order of service': there seems to have been some structure to what went on. But they had a structure that allowed for silence (so they could hear God speak) and spontaneity (so that someone could have the freedom to speak out God's word). Would that we might give the Spirit of God more room in our services! Of course we still need prepared teaching, but some of our services are so one hundred per cent predictable that we are not in all honesty open to the moving of God.

● *They put God's word into practice.* When they were convinced that God had called two of their top men, they were obedient to his word and released them (Acts 13:2–3). That took courage on the part of the leadership and the church ('Our best men can't go – how will we manage without them?' doesn't seem to have figured much). They prayed for their brothers, meaning business with God. They acted in obedience to God, whatever the sacrifice meant to them.

● *Their care was real.* As we have already noticed, they cared about new believers (Acts 11:23). As the church consisted of Jews and Gentiles, they must have had to learn to care for each other as well. They also cared about the hungry and poor – so much so that they gave spontaneously when they heard that a famine was coming to the Christians in Jerusalem (Acts 11:27–30). Do you remember Galatians 6:10: 'Do good to all people,

especially to those who belong to the family of believers'?
Do you and I practise it?

The practice of tithing, generally speaking, doesn't get
a good press – but I like the clear promise of God in
Malachi 3:10: 'Bring the whole tithe into the storehouse,
that there may be food in my house. Test me in this . . .
and see if I will not throw open the floodgates of heaven
and pour out so much blessing that you will not have
room enough for it.' Sir Fred Catherwood (in *God's Time,
God's Money*) recalls a time when he preached on tithing
and comments that the congregation 'couldn't get out of
the door fast enough. If I caught anyone's eye, I got a
shifty look and a curt "Goodnight".' Sometimes the truth
can get too uncomfortably practical!

The church at Antioch, then, looked beyond itself. They
may well have already been thinking about spreading the
gospel elsewhere when God's call came to them. As
Michael Green writes, 'I doubt if they would have even
listened to the Spirit on the missionary call had they not
already been thinking about the folk who needed to hear
the gospel not only in Antioch but beyond. But they did
have the interest, and when the call came they heeded it.'
Is your church enthusiastic for mission? Is mine? Or do we
leave 'mission' to the zealous few and one special weekend a
year?

> Facing a task unfinished,
>   That drives us to our knees,
> A need that, undiminished,
>   Rebukes our slothful ease,
> We, who rejoice to know Thee,
>   Renew before Thy throne
> The solemn pledge we owe Thee
>   To go and make Thee known.

Where other lords beside Thee
  Hold their unhindered sway,
Where forces that defied Thee
  Defy Thee still today,
With none to heed their crying
  For life, and love, and light,
Unnumbered souls are dying,
  And pass into the night.

We bear the torch that flaming
  Fell from the hands of those
Who gave their lives proclaiming
  That Jesus died and rose.
Ours is the same commission,
  The same glad message ours,
Fired by the same ambition,
  To Thee we yield our powers.

O Father who sustained them,
  O Spirit who inspired,
Saviour, whose love constrained them
  To toil with zeal untired,
From cowardice defend us,
  From lethargy awake!
Forth on Thine errands send us
  To labour for Thy sake.

Frank Houghton, 1894–1972

Conclusion

Everyone involved; breaking new ground for the gospel; shared, realistic leadership; dynamic worship that led to a practical caring for one another and a lost world: Lord Jesus, make our church more like the church at Antioch!

'The disciples were called Christians first at Antioch' (Acts 11:26).

4

THE SERVICES OF THE CHURCH

Key thought In the church we experience the reality of belonging to God and his family. We worship God together; we share our lives together.

Key Bible verse 'Let us not give up meeting together, as some are in the habit of doing, but let us encourage one another – and all the more as you see the Day approaching' (Hebrews 10:25).

The benefits of meeting together

When we're spiritually down, sometimes the last thing we want is other Christians around us. We want to be by ourselves. Perhaps it was this that the writer to the discouraged Hebrew Christians had in mind when he reminded them to get together for true encouragement (Hebrews 10:24–25).

What happens when we meet together? The Bible says that Jesus himself draws near to us in a special way (Matthew 18:20). We can sense this in our worship of God.

Our privilege: enjoying God

We may be able to remember the words of the Shorter Catechism, 'Man's chief end is to glorify God and to enjoy him forever' but I wonder if we know so much about what it means to enjoy God as we do about glorifying him. When we worship God, we enjoy him: our response to him expresses itself in praise and adoration. This is, in fact, something very natural. Read the words of C. S. Lewis (*Reflections on the Psalms*): 'I had never noticed that all enjoyment spontaneously overflows into praise unless (sometimes even if) shyness or the fear of boring others is deliberately brought in to check it. The world rings with praise – lovers praising their mistresses, readers their favourite poet, walkers praising the countryside, players praising their favourite game – praise of weather, wines, dishes, actors, motors, horses, colleges, countries, historical personages, children, flowers, mountains, rare stamps, rare beetles, even sometimes politicians or scholars. I had not noticed how the humblest, and at the same time most balanced and capacious, minds, praised most, while the cranks, misfits and malcontents praised least. I had not noticed either that just as men spontaneously praise whatever they value, so they spontaneously urge us to join them in praising it: "Isn't she lovely? Wasn't it glorious? Don't you think that magnificent?" The Psalmists in telling everyone to praise God are doing what all men do when they speak of what they care about.'

Worship is when we give God the honour due to his name. 'The language "fabulous", "fantastic", "smashing" is the language of spontaneous praise in recognition of worth-ship. That's worship!' (Michael Griffiths, *Cinderella with Amnesia*). When was the last time you and I thought or uttered words such as those? When were we last truly 'lost in wonder, love, and praise'?

Enter: the Spirit of God

'The grand thing the church wants in this time is God's Holy Spirit. You will get up plans and say, "Now if the church were altered a little bit, it would go on better." You think that if there were different ministers, or different church order, or something different, then all would be well. No, dear friends, it is not there that the mistake lies; it is that we want more of the Spirit . . . That is the church's great want, and until that want be supplied, we may reform, and reform, and still be just the same. All we want is the Spirit of God.' When do you think these words were written? 1980? 1970? No, 1857: they are the words of Charles Spurgeon. We saw on pp. 71–110 how the Spirit energizes and vitalizes God's people. He does this in the church's worship. His activity may be seen in the gifts of the Spirit (1 Corinthians 12, 14); his activity is also seen in the way he works through the less spectacular, but no less important ongoing services of the church.

The church's services

• *Teaching and preaching the truth.* Jesus said, 'If you hold to my teaching, you are really my disciples. Then you will know the truth, and the truth will set you free' (John 8:31–32). One central aim of the church is to defend the truth (1 Timothy 3:15; Jude 3). This means proclaiming truth and condemning error (2 Timothy 3:16). And the whole of Scripture is important – not just our own pet hobby-horse or emphases (Acts 20:27).

• *Prayer.* 'When he [Jesus] saw the crowds, he had compassion on them, because they were harassed and helpless, like sheep without a shepherd. Then he said to his disciples, "The harvest is plentiful but the workers are few. Ask the Lord of the harvest, therefore, to send out workers into his harvest field" ' (Matthew 9:36–38). Faced with the matter of evangelism, Jesus' first priority here was prayer, not organization. Corporate prayer is the power-house of a church. Unspectacular, hard work it may be, but if we neglect it, then we should not be surprised if our churches are weak and our evangelism lacking in fruit.

- *The special services ('ordinances') of baptism and communion.* These were both instituted by Jesus as outward visible signs of inward spiritual realities.

  ☐ Baptism marks the entry into God's church. Baptizing is included in Jesus' commission to make disciples of all nations (Matthew 28:19). The meaning of baptism is a death to the old life and a rising to new life. It means that the person who is being baptized has been crucified with Christ, and that the life of sin is a thing of the past. The rising to the new life speaks of being raised with Christ to walk in the light with him (Romans 6:1–11).

  ☐ In holy communion (or the Lord's supper), the bread and wine stand for Christ's body and blood, given for us in his death (Matthew 26:26–29). The marks of this fellowship meal are simplicity and reverence (1 Corinthians 11:23–29). We remember he died for us. We thank the risen Christ for what he means to us personally. We receive God's grace, strength, and help in a fresh way for the now of our lives. We share in the meal with other members of our Christian family. We look forward to his coming again.

Real fellowship

What does the idea of fellowship suggest to you? A group of Christians talking together with other believers at the end of a meeting? A cup of tea at the end of service? A Christian holiday abroad? Important though these social events may be, they need not necessarily be fellowship. True Christian fellowship has to do with sharing. Sharing first of all in a 'vertical' dimension – with God; and then in a 'horizontal' dimension – with others. 'Our fellowship is with the Father and with his Son, Jesus Christ' (1 John 1:3, the vertical dimension); 'fellowship with one another' (1 John 1:7, the horizontal dimension). We enter into fellowship with God by receiving for ourselves the benefits of Christ's death for us. Fellowship with other Christians helps us enjoy a full relationship with God. We are back at Hebrews 10:24–25 again: 'Let us consider how we may spur one another on towards love and good deeds. Let us not give up meeting together, as some are in the habit of doing, but let us encourage one another.'

Christian fellowship is a matter of giving and receiving, and we all need both. Look again at the early church (Acts 2:42–47). And even the apostle Paul didn't just want to serve people all the time: he knew he needed encouragement from other Christians (Romans 1:12; 15:32). We may be always on the receiving end of others' kindness, never actually doing anything ourselves. That is lop-sided; we need a balance of serving others and receiving from them. Fellowship is something that is two-way.

To be practical . . .

How can these thoughts about the church's services be translated into reality, in a life that is for many very busy? Some suggestions:

- *Make the most of the time*. We all know time is precious. Some are made to feel guilty if they are not at an 'important' service or Christian meeting. Quite often, special meetings are arranged on Saturdays – a day many want to spend with their families. So: here is a plea to make the most of the time that is at our disposal. Perhaps this is a plea to be more organized in our own personal life. It certainly is a plea to use the time that we are together as believers more properly. We need to encourage one another more positively in informal times at the end of services, or in house groups. We need to see more true fellowship and strengthening one another in a real way to go on with God.

- *Review our commitments and church programmes*. It can be helpful to review our own involvement in different spheres of service. Do we really need to be on the committee for this and leader of that? I'm sure there should be an examination and, where appropriate, some 'stream-lining' of the regular meetings of a church to examine their effectiveness. Perhaps such an examination would allow greater time for church members to spend with their families.

- *Work out the reality that we need each other.* There is a danger, particularly, for leaders, that we can think we are self-sufficient – that we don't need others' help. Whoever we are, new Christian or older, we may be too proud, or always on the defensive, or jealous of others, or just plain cool towards those around us. Yet our lives will be all the weaker without fellowship. It can be good to have one particular Christian friend with whom we can share our lives regularly. Showing hospitality by inviting others from church to our home is a good way to get to know others more.

    Jim Packer was asked if he would want to include anything new in his book *Knowing God* when preparing its Study Guide. There were no 'omissions in terms of the overall plan'. 'But one defect I do see. In addressing my readers as individuals, trying as best I can to single them out and search their hearts before God, I fail to show that it is only as one gives oneself in human relationships, in the home, in friendships, with neigh-bours, as members of Christian groups and teams – in relationships that go sometimes right and sometimes wrong, as all our relationships do – that experiential knowledge of God becomes real and deep. For ordinary people, to be a hermit is *not* the way! The buttoned-up Christian "loner" who keeps aloof and reads books like this (or just the Bible!) may pick up true notions of God as well as anyone else may – but only the Christian sharer, who risks being hurt in order to take and give the maximum in fellowship and who sometimes does get hurt as a result, ever knows much of God himself in experiential terms. This perspective ... is so vital that I am very much at fault for not having made more of it.' We all need each other.

> Jesus, we look to Thee,
>   Thy promised presence claim;
> Thou in the midst of us shalt be,
>   Assembled in Thy Name.
>
> Thy Name salvation is,
>   Which here we come to prove;
> Thy Name is life, and health, and peace,
>   And everlasting love.
>
> We meet, the grace to take
>   Which Thou hast freely given;
> We meet on earth for Thy dear sake,
>   That we may meet in heaven.
>
> Present we know Thou art,
>   But O Thyself reveal!
> Now, Lord, let every bounding heart
>   The mighty comfort feel.
>
> O may Thy quickening voice
>   The death of sin remove;
> And bid our inmost souls rejoice
>   In hope of perfect love!
>
>   Charles Wesley, 1707–88

Conclusion

Are there positive steps we can take to make our worship of God more honouring to him? And are there also steps we can take to make our fellowship with others in the church more helpful and encouraging?

'For where two or three come together in my name, there am I with them' (Jesus, in Matthew 18:20).

5

THE MISSION OF THE CHURCH

> *Key thought* A healthy church is one that is concerned about missionary work on its own doorstep and abroad.
>
> *Key Bible verse* 'Go and make disciples of all nations, baptising them in the name of the Father and of the Son and of the Holy Spirit, and teaching them to obey everything I have commanded you. And surely I am with you always, to the very end of the age' (Jesus, in Matthew 28:19–20).

Before Jesus ascended to heaven, he gave his disciples a specific command: 'Go and make disciples of all nations, baptising them in the name of the Father and of the Son and of the Holy Spirit, and teaching them to obey everything I have commanded you' (Matthew 28:19–20). This commission is to be fulfilled by the church in every age.

Let us ask two basic questions about the mission of the church.

Why?

Why should we be involved in mission?
- Because of who God is.
  - ☐ The Father's love (John 3:16; Romans 8:32; 1 John 3:16; 4:10).
  - ☐ The command and promise of the Lord Jesus Christ (Matthew 18:18–20; Acts 1:8).
  - ☐ The thrust of the Holy Spirit's power (Acts 1:6–8).

• Because of the world's needs. We only have to watch the television news or read our newspapers to see the moral disasters facing the world. People are 'perishing', they 'love darkness instead of light', and 'do evil' (John 3:16–20). Look at Ephesians 2. Those who are not Christians are spiritually dead and without hope (verses 1–2, 12); they are under God's anger (verse 3) unless and until God steps in in mercy and grace (verses 4–5) leading them to faith (verse 8). But such a response can only be made by those who hear the good news – which means someone must tell it to them (Romans 10:14–15).

How?

How is our mission to the world to be expressed?

• Through prayer. Jesus' compassion for lost and helpless people led him to prayer (Matthew 9:36–38).

When we pray, we lay hold of the person of God. We come in touch with him. Look at Acts 4:23–31. The main concern of the believers here is not with the opposition they had just gone through and would expect to meet again. Rather, most of the prayer is taken up with God – and his sovereign control over events (verses 24–28). It is only later (verse 29) that they bring their own personal situation before God. In prayer, we are to see God's priorities, his perspective, what is on his heart.

When we pray, we lay hold of the power of God. The believers prayed not for comfort, but for boldness. And God moved in power (verse 31). In prayer, we acknowledge our weakness and ask God for the courage and confidence given by his Spirit.

• Through action. Prayer is not a substitute for action (end of verse 31). What did they do? They were involved with people; they were committed to people. To use John Stott's phrase, they were holy and worldly: 'The church is a people that is simultaneously holy (distinct from the world because belonging to God) and worldly in the sense of being immersed in the life of the people around it' (John 17:11, 14–18) ... 'Mission arises from the biblical doctrine of the church in the world. If we are not the holy people of God, hearing and passing on his word, we shall have nothing to say because we are compromised. But if we are not simultaneously in the world we shall have no-one to serve' (*Today* magazine).

So what does this mean practically? The examples of Jesus and the early church show us a genuine caring for people in both word and deed (e.g. Mark 1:40–41; 2:1–12; 1 John 3:17–18). As individuals in the church we are to proclaim words (Acts 4:31; 8:4–5) and we are to perform good deeds as well (Acts 6:1–2; 8:6–7). Both evangelism (words) and service (actions) are part of our mission to the world.

For me, the key is love. When we are genuine with people – when it is quite clear that we are not out to see how many converts we can notch up as status symbols of our Christian life, when we are natural with people in every sphere of our lives at work, home, etc., then we will be open to seeing the needs of those around us. We will 'build bridges' and over a period of time opportunities will arise to say what Jesus means to us, and some of our friends may become Christians.

Our action doesn't end when our friends (for that is what they will have become as we have shared our lives with them, 1 Thessalonians 2:8) become Christians. We need to nurture them in their new-found faith, by care (1 Thessalonians 2:7), example (1 Thessalonians 1:6), and prayer (Philippians 1:4–6). The friendship and encouragement of older believers helped me inestimably in my first two years as a new Christian. Encouraging a deeper understanding of the gospel, a sense of assurance – based on facts (e.g. John 6:37; 10:28–29), not feelings – and offering practical guidance on some of the 'hows' of being a Christian (How can I get into the Bible? How can I stop my mind drifting when I pray?) and life in the church (baptism, church membership, giving time and money) are all important.

Getting involved in mission

Mission, then, includes evangelism and service in Jesus' name at home and abroad: this seems to be the thrust of Jesus' words in Acts 1:8. How can such a greater sense of mission be inspired in our churches?

- By prayer – for God to revive his church, to help us see that people are going to hell unless they respond to Jesus. We need to be stirred up again with the love of Jesus for a lost world.

- By teaching – that mission is not on the periphery of the life of the church but at its heart. Mission isn't up to the enthusiastic few who choose it as an optional extra, but it's the responsibility of all the church membership.

- By sharing a vision – that is strongly felt by the leadership: 'Unless the minister sees the need to make mission central, unless the leaders are well motivated, it is hard to make any progress' (Michael Griffiths, *Ten Sending Churches*).

- By information – regular, up-to-date information of what God is doing. Regular sharing of information in a church service (e.g. by praying for a country using the *Operation World* handbook) can be a good way to develop a church's global vision. This may be more helpful than leaving prayer letters and literature from missionary societies to gather dust at the back of churches.

- By challenge – to commit ourselves to get involved with what God is doing. Under God, we will then become more involved ourselves in God's work and surely we will see some commit themselves to new avenues of service for God.

We have heard the joyful sound:
   Jesus saves!
Spread the tidings all around:
   Jesus saves!
Bear the news to every land,
   Climb the steeps and cross the waves;
Onward! 'tis our Lord's command:
   Jesus saves!

Sing above the battle's strife:
   Jesus saves!
By His death and endless life,
   Jesus saves!
Sing it softly through the gloom,
   When the heart for mercy craves;
Sing in triumph o'er the tomb:
   Jesus saves!

Give the winds a mighty voice:
   Jesus saves!
Let the nations now rejoice:
   Jesus saves!
Shout salvation full and free,
   Highest hills and deepest caves;
This our song of victory:
   Jesus saves!

Priscilla Jane Owens, 1829–1907

Conclusion

'A Christian who is not dedicated to world evangelism is living an unbiblical life, and a church that is not dedicated to missionary vision is an unbiblical church' (Pete Lowman).

'You will be my witnesses in Jerusalem, and in all Judea and Samaria, and to the ends of the earth' (Jesus, in Acts 1:8).

6

THE WARFARE OF THE CHURCH

Key thought One of the pictures that the New Testament uses to describe the church is that of an *army* – an army engaged in a spiritual battle.

Key Bible verse 'Your enemy the devil prowls around like a roaring lion looking for someone to devour. Resist him, standing firm in the faith, because you know that your brothers throughout the world are undergoing the same kind of sufferings' (1 Peter 5:8–9).

The Lord Jesus warned us of 'trouble in the world' (John 16:33); Paul and Barnabas told new disciples, 'We must go through many hardships to enter the kingdom of God' (Acts 14:22). 'Why should it be like this? The fact is that when we become Christians, we enter not a holiday camp where everything is jolly and comfortable, but rather a battle station in the middle of a fierce war. We are now soldiers in the Lord's army, and the enemy exerts tremendous pressure upon us' (Peter Jeffery, *Stand firm*).

Our enemy

Our enemy is the devil (Ephesians 6:11) – the one behind all the evil in the world. His one aim is to oppose God and his works. The whole world is under his control (1 John 5:19). He is called 'the god of this age' (2 Corinthians 4:4), 'the ruler of the kingdom of the air' (Ephesians 2:2), 'the one who leads the whole world astray' (Revelation 12:9). His actions include originating lies and being a murderer (John 8:44) and accusing believers (Revelation 12:10). He disguises himself as an angel of light (2 Corinthians 11:13–15). He is like a roaring lion (1 Peter 5:8–9). He is crafty and cunning (Genesis 3:1; 2 Corinthians 11:3); he will try to outwit us (2 Corinthians 2:11) and set up traps for us to fall into (1 Timothy 3:7; 2 Timothy 2:26).

On the cross, God in Christ broke the hold that the devil had on mankind (Colossians 2:13–15; Hebrews 2:14–15). This means that when we become Christians, not only are our sins forgiven, but the old control that the devil had over us (John 8:44; 1 John 3:10) has been broken. We are no longer slaves to sin; we have died to sin (Romans 6:1–11).

The devil does not stand idly by, however. Although he cannot regain complete power over Christians, he tries to make our lives very difficult.

Our action

Do we give in, in the face of such a great opposer? No, 'the evil one cannot harm him [the Christian]' (1 John 5:18). We should be careful of Satan, but needn't be scared out of our wits by him. Our task is to resist him, and to stay close to Jesus (James 4:7; 1 Peter 5:8–9). How, practically, can we do this?

Paul's passage on spiritual warfare in Ephesians 6:10–20 is worthy of closer study.

• Our strength is in God. Our own strength is nothing (John 15:5). So where is our strength? In God (Ephesians 6:10; all other references in this section beginning 'verse' refer to Ephesians 6:10–20). Not so much in any abilities, organization, or enthusiasm we may have, but in the infinite resources of almighty God!

The instructions in this passage are in the plural.

Although there will be constant individual skirmishes, it is *together* that we stand against the devil's schemes. It is *together* that we are to be strong in the Lord. That is why the relationships amongst believers must be protected.

● Stand! (verses 11, 13, 14) In other words don't give in, don't surrender!

● Put on the full armour of God (verses 11, 13). All the armour is needed – one part of the armour protects one part of the body, another part, another part of the body. Notice, too, that it is all *God's* armour. What, then, is the armour?

☐ The belt of truth (verse 14). This refers to our sincerity, our genuineness. Are we truly sincere about spiritual warfare? It also refers to our knowledge of the truth: the Bible. Do we have an unqualified confidence in the truth of the Bible?

☐ The breastplate of righteousness (verse 14). This is God's righteousness – which is credited to us by Christ's death through justification (Romans 4:3–6) – and the righteousness that is the work of the Holy Spirit making us more like Jesus. With this righteousness on, we cannot live with inconsistencies in our lives. Are we living in a right relationship with God and other people (Acts 24:16)? Or is there bitterness, distrust, or resentment in our lives?

☐ Feet fitted with the readiness . . . from the gospel of peace (verse 15). A Roman soldier's heavy sandals gave him firmness – he wouldn't slide around all over the place – and mobility. God's people are to be a people on the go. The gospel brings peace to our hearts and stirs us to share the good news with others courageously. Or do we prefer to put our feet up and just take things easy in life?

☐ The shield of faith (verse 16). We now come to the second group of three pieces of armour. It is as if the first three are to be on all the time. 'But when you come to the second group there is a suggestion immediately of activity. The soldier may be sitting down in his room in the barracks and taking a period of rest, but he still keeps on his girdle of truth, his breastplate and his sandals. Then suddenly an alarm is given that the enemy is already attacking, and he immediately takes hold of his shield and his sword and puts on his helmet and rushes out. There is the suggestion of activity, of an actual fight and battle' (D. M. Lloyd-Jones).

The shield of faith can be compared to the present-day police riot shield. When police stand next to one another with their shields in position, they form a solid wall that stops all missiles that are hurled. An individual on his or her own is extremely vulnerable, but in a group the shields make a single line of defence. So it is with us: we *need* other believers in the spiritual battles we're fighting – it isn't God's intention that we fight our lonely battles.

What are the flaming arrows? Charles Hodge comments helpfully: 'It is a common experience of the people of God that at times horrible thoughts, unholy, blasphemous, sceptical, malignant, crowd upon the mind, which cannot be accounted for on any ordinary law of mental action, and which cannot be dislodged. They stick like burning arrows; and fill the soul with agony. They can be quenched only by faith; by calling on Christ for help. These, however, are not the only kind of fiery darts; nor are they the most dangerous. There are others which enkindle passion, inflame ambition, excite cupidity [greedy desire for money and possessions], pride, discontent, or vanity; producing a flame which our deceitful heart is not so prompt to extinguish, and which is often allowed to burn until it produces great injury and even destruction. Against these most dangerous weapons of the evil one, the only protection is faith.'

It is when we take up the shield of faith (1 John 5:4), when we apply what we know of God and his grace in the battle we're engaged in, that the arrows are put out. 'Do not be afraid, Abram. I am your shield,' said God to Abraham (Genesis 15:1).

□ The helmet of salvation (verse 17). The helmet protects our brain, our mind – where we remind ourselves of the greatness of our salvation. This is to stop us from becoming weary and discouraged. We are to be confident in the certain 'hope of salvation' (1 Thessalonians 5:8). Are our minds guarded by God's salvation? Do we keep our eyes fixed on God, not so much on our present difficulties, but on his perspective? What awaits us is an eternal glory (2 Corinthians 4:7–18).

□ The sword of the Spirit (verse 17). This is the only offensive weapon; all the other items mentioned are pieces of defensive armour. What is the sword of the Spirit? It is the word of God (end of verse 17): the Bible. The Holy Spirit is the author of Scripture (2 Peter 1:21). The word of God has deep, penetrating effects (Hebrews 4:12). We are to use it when facing temptations (Matthew 4:3–11) and to release others from the control of the enemy (2 Corinthians 10:4). How well do we know our Bibles? And do we use such knowledge in the battle?

□ Prayer (verses 18–20). Prayer, strictly speaking, is not part of the armour – but it is an absolute must if we are to succeed in the battle. All the armour may be in the right place, but do we still depend on God himself? In the midst of life's battles do we pray? Do we pray with other believers?

> Soldiers of Christ, arise,
>   And put your armour on;
> Strong in the strength which God supplies,
>   Through His eternal Son;
> Strong in the Lord of hosts,
>   And in His mighty power;
> Who in the strength of Jesus trusts
>   Is more than conqueror.

Stand, then, in His great might,
   With all His strength endued;
And take, to arm you for the fight,
   The panoply of God.
To keep your armour bright
   Attend with constant care,
Still serving in your Captain's sight,
   And watching unto prayer.

From strength to strength go on;
   Wrestle and fight and pray;
Tread all the powers of darkness down,
   And win the well-fought day;
That, having all things done,
   And all your conflicts past,
Ye may o'ercome through Christ alone,
   And stand complete at last.

                              Charles Wesley, 1707–88

Conclusion

Victory is certain: we are involved because we are Christians, but, most importantly, the battle is the Lord's not ours.

'Put on the full armour of God so that you can take your stand against the devil's schemes' (Ephesians 6:11).

7

THE UNITY OF THE CHURCH

Key thought All true Christians are already one; this unity, based on truth, needs to be worked out in a spirit of love in our churches.

Key Bible verse 'You are all sons of God through faith in Christ Jesus, for all of you who were baptised into Christ have clothed yourselves with Christ. There is neither Jew not Greek, slave nor free, male nor female, for you are all one in Christ Jesus' (Galatians 3:26–28).

What is unity?

Unity is exciting! It is one of the gifts God gives his people (Ephesians 4:3; 1 Corinthians 12:13). The oneness that already exists in a group of believers is something real: it reflects the very relationship that exists between the persons of the Trinity (John 17:21–22). Note that such a unity is something spiritual, not organizational.

In John chapter 17, Jesus longs for those who accept his words, those who believe (verse 8), to be truly one. He wants those who respond to the gospel, who are true believers in himself, to be united. Such a unity is based on truth (verse 17). There are central matters of biblical truth that Christians must hold on to at all costs – certain non-negotiable truths. These truths include the facts that Jesus was both fully God and fully man, that he died on the cross to forgive our sins, that he rose again, and that he promises eternal life to all those who trust him. There are some secondary matters on which Christians have different view-points. There must be room to accept these. As has been said, 'In necessary things, unity; in doubtful things, liberty; in all things, charity.' So when we come to disagreements, let's not get disagreeable! Let's remember that God has put us in *his* church (1 Corinthians 3:1–9).

All are one in Christ Jesus

In the church, all really *are* one (Galatians 3:28). Barriers, be they racial or religious (Jew and Greek), social (slave and free), or sexual (male and female) are to be abandoned, since in Christ all are equal. This is not to say that all are the same. No, the Bible teaches a diversity within this unity (1 Corinthians 12) and this diversity of members is to be respected (1 Corinthians 12:15–26).

The effects of disunity

Disunity spoils. It spoils the life and witness of a local church, breaking up relationships. Disunity also weakens the work of God within the world. As Festo Kivengere put it, 'By our denominationalism we tell the world how much we hate each other.'

Unity begins at home

Church unity is discussed by committees, but like charity, unity must really begin to be worked at and worked out at home. We must ask ourselves, 'How united are we as a church?' Let's put some of Paul's encouragements on unity into questions:

- Are we standing firm in one spirit, contending as one man for the faith of the gospel (Philippians 1:27)?

- Are we making every effort to keep the unity already given by the Spirit by means of the peace that binds us together (Ephesians 4:3)?

• Are we humble and gentle, patient, and tolerant with
  another in a loving manner (Ephesians 4:2)?

Unity grows on (and in) you

If we answer these questions honestly, we'll probably realize that we've a long way to go. But if we realize that, then
at least we've made a start. Because unity is something
that grows. It involves all of us 'pulling our weight', putting
into practice the gifts God has given us to reach maturity
(Ephesians 4:11–16).

• Unity is the point when there is blessing (Psalm 133).

• It is where Jesus reveals himself and prayers are
  answered (Matthew 18:19–20).

• It is the place where God moves (Acts 2; 4:32–35).

What is the ultimate purpose of unity? It isn't to make us
inward-looking, constantly taken up with ourselves. The
real purpose is that the world may know that God is the
God of love who sent Jesus into the world (John 17:21,
23). As John White puts it, 'The church that convinces
men that there is a God in heaven is a church that manifests
what only a heavenly God can do, that is, to unite human
beings in heavenly love. Wherever the sign of loving unity
exists, the world will be convinced. Miracles of healing,
large mass rallies, powerful preaching, superb organization
all may have their place. But there is nothing on earth
which convinces men about heaven or that awakens their
craving for it like the discovery of Christian brothers who
love one another.'

Expressing unity

Unity – within a church or between churches – develops
where there is trust: honesty and openness, rather than
suspicion and hostility. We will need to accept and respect

some differences in an atmosphere of love, not dishonestly papering over the cracks that divide. In working together on a joint project, for example an inter-church evangelistic mission, healthier relationships develop, too.

May God, the source of unity, give us a spirit of unity as we follow Jesus, so that as one we will glorify him (Romans 15:5–6)!

> Lord from whom all blessings flow,
> Perfecting the church below,
> Steadfast may we cleave to Thee,
> Love, the mystic union be;
> Join our faithful spirits, join
> Each to each, and all to Thine;
> Lead us through the paths of peace
> On to perfect holiness.
>
> Move and actuate and guide;
> Divers gifts to each divide;
> Placed according to Thy will,
> Let us all our work fulfil;
> Never from our office move;
> Needful to each other prove;
> Use the grace on each bestowed,
> Tempered by the art of God.
>
> Sweetly may we all agree,
> Touched with softest sympathy;
> There is neither bond nor free,
> Great nor servile, Lord, in Thee:
> Love, like death, hath all destroyed,
> Rendered all distinctions void;
> Names and sects and parties fall,
> Thou, O Christ, art All in all.
>
> Charles Wesley, 1707–88

Conclusion

Christians who are agreed on the basic truths of the gospel, even though they worship in different churches, can present a powerful witness to their community.

'My prayer . . . is that all of them may be one, Father, just as you are in me and I am in you . . . so that the world may believe that you have sent me' (Jesus, in John 17:20–21).

8

WORKING IT OUT

Glory in the church

Where does all our thinking about the church take us to?

'Glory in the church and in Christ Jesus' (Ephesians 3:21)

May glory – adoration and praise – be shown to God in the church and the head of the church, for his power, love, and wisdom! Perhaps in reading through these pages we have come to see again that the church is the church of Jesus Christ. *He* is the one who is building his church. Glory will be given to God in a church where there is:
- inspired proclamation of the Bible;
- genuine, spiritual worship (and when all come prepared for this!);
- heart-felt prayer;
- true fellowship and love amongst the church members;
- a deep concern to spread the gospel.

'With all the saints' (Ephesians 3:18)

Our thinking about the church may also have led us to see that we aren't meant to exist just as individual Christians. How can I come to know more of God? By myself? Yes, certainly, a little. But surely I get to know him much, much more 'with all the saints', when some of the barriers of my life and theirs have come down, where we have come to see our real selves and so can truly love and encourage one another.

So the church isn't an awkward, ugly, inefficient part of God's purposes – the church is utterly central to God's plan for the world. The church is people, a people redeemed by the blood of the Lamb, a people getting ready to be a bride, surely the most beautiful bride ever seen (Ephesians 5:25–27; Revelation 21:1–4). The wonder – and privilege – is ours to be involved, to make the church into a warm living community, to see that all of God's people are got into a fit state to do works of loving service, in order that the body of Christ will be built up (Ephesians 4:12). It'll mean 'getting our hands dirty', it'll mean being misunderstood, it'll mean a great deal of hard work, but it'll be worth it, as it's working out the reality of being the people of God in our own day and age.

> 'Now to him who is able to do immeasurably more than all we ask or imagine, according to his power that is at work within us, to him be glory in the church and in Christ Jesus throughout all generations, for ever and ever! Amen!' (Ephesians 3:20–21).

Living in the world

1

ENJOYING GOD'S WORD

Key thought The Bible has been given to us to change the way in which we live in the world.

Key Bible verse 'All Scripture is God-breathed and is useful for teaching, rebuking, correcting and training in righteousness, so that the man of God may be thoroughly equipped for every good work' (2 Timothy 3:16–17).

It might seem strange to begin our section on living in the world with considering God's word, the Bible. And yet, after all, why do we read our Bibles? To know of God, to know of his thoughts. But to what purpose? So that we can become walking encyclopedias of Bible facts? No! So that we can know God and so be the kind of people he wants us to be in the world. So what does the Bible say about itself?

- The Bible is like a judge (Hebrews 4:12). The Bible discerns the intentions and dispositions within us. It passes judgment on 'what makes us tick'. Don't we sometimes know this uncomfortable uncovering of wrong in our lives as we listen to a sermon or as we read our

Bibles on our own? The Bible as judge reminds us too that we are not to criticize the Bible, destructively laying aside the bits that we don't like. Rather, we are to submit to him from whose sight 'nothing in all creation is hidden' and 'to whom we must give account' (Hebrews 4:13).

- The Bible is like a shower of rain (Deuteronomy 32:2; 2 Samuel 23:2–4). The Scriptures refresh and revive us! Aren't there dry times in our lives when we need God to break up the barrenness by the renewing of the Spirit-inspired work of God?

  The picture of the rain causing growth is found in Isaiah 55:10–11: God's word *will* surely do its work, often gradually and quietly, fulfilling his purposes.

- The Bible is like a seed (Luke 8:11; 1 Peter 1:23). The promise here is of fruitfulness. We are to sow the seed (Ecclesiastes 11:6; 2 Corinthians 9:6); the responsibility for growth is God's (1 Corinthians 3:6). We can be confident that the seed is living (Mark 4:26–29). What joy there is at harvest (Psalm 126:6)!

- The Bible is like a sword (Ephesians 6:17; Hebrews 4:12). We looked at this when we thought about spiritual warfare (see p. 145). The sword is the weapon we use as soldiers against our spiritual enemies. It is double-edged (Hebrews 4:12). As Herbert Lockyer comments, 'it can cut both ways. If the Bible does not save, then it slays. If it fails to convert, then it condemns (Acts 2:37, 41; 7:51, 54, 57).' It will convict and convert, or it will harden the heart, yet leaving us without excuse.

- The Bible is like a hammer (Jeremiah 23:29). Hearts of those who resist the gospel are hard. Our task is to keep on using God's hammer, praying that God will use it to crack open rock-like hearts so that his life can burst in. Hammers are also used to smooth and shape objects (Isaiah 41:7): the Bible fashions our lives to God's plan.

As believers our hearts can become hardened (Hebrews 3:12). This distresses our Saviour greatly (Mark 3:5). May we encourage each other to have hearts that are constantly sensitive to God (Hebrews 3:13). And may we humble ourselves before God, repenting from any sin in our lives and keeping close to him (Hebrews 3:12).

• The Bible is like a fire (Jeremiah 20:9; 23:29). Fire symbolizes God's presence and holiness (Exodus 3:1–6). The Bible, as fire, is to destroy all that is wrong in my life; it is to refine me. The power of fire is seen with the disciples at Pentecost: 'words from their tongues of fire burned their way into the cold hearts of multitudes'. And how I long more and more to know my heart burning within me as the Scriptures are opened up (Luke 24:32)!

• The Bible is like a lamp (Psalm 119:105, 130). Which of us does not need daily light to guide us through life? We need to remember that this is something serious – it's not like children playing around with a torch in the dark. We need light to dispel the darkness both of the fallen world that we live in, separated from God by sin (John 3:19) and of our natural human hearts (2 Corinthians 4:6). Light shows up the dirt, and so makes clearing up any rubbish in our lives possible; 'we will do well to pay attention' to God's word, therefore (2 Peter 1:19). As Michael Green comments, 'We are on pilgrimage throughout our lives in this dark world. God has graciously provided us with a lamp, the Scriptures. If we pay attention to them for reproof, warning, guidance and encouragement we shall walk safely. If we neglect them, we shall be engulfed by darkness. The whole course of our lives ought to be governed by the Word of God.'

• The Bible is like a mirror (James 1:22–25). A mirror reveals and reflects. When we stand before a mirror, we see ourselves as we really are, warts and all. Mirrors don't lie – except for those mirrors at circuses or fun-fairs that give distortions! 'The promise of a perfect reve-lation of God and ourselves is ours when we accept the Bible as the divine mirror' (Herbert Lockyer). Again the promise is practical – do we look into a mirror and then just forget about what we see? No, we act on what we see – adjusting our hair, clothes, posture, etc. Similarly, the Bible calls us not just to be casual passive listeners or readers but *doers* (read James 1:22–25 again). And if we act on what we see, we shall gradually be changed to be like Jesus (2 Corinthians 3:18).

- The Bible cleans us up. The book that shows up my sin, as in a mirror, is also the way of cleaning me up (Ephes-ians 5:26). Here the 'washing with water' is baptism. The washing of water in connection with the word, the Bible (Ephesians 6:17), cleanses and sanctifies us. This takes place when we become Christians and goes on throughout our lives. So God's word is there to make us holy (John 17:17) and pure (Psalm 119:9).

- The Bible is like food.
    The Bible is like milk – so that babes, be they people who are young in physical years (2 Timothy 3:15) or spiritual experience, can drink in truth and grow (1 Corinthians 3:2; Hebrews 5:12–13; 1 Peter 2:2). But as babies are weaned and move on to solids, so we are to go deeper with God in our Christian life.
    The Bible is like meat (Hebrews 5:12–14). This is for those who want to really 'get their teeth into' God's truth. And taking in the solid meat of God's word isn't something heavy and dull.
    The Bible is like bread (Matthew 4:4). We need daily bread, daily sustenance – and not just a few meagre crumbs, but several nourishing slices of God's strength-ening word to satisfy our hunger. How much of God's word are we taking in?

The Bible is sweeter than honey (Psalm 19:10; 119:103). When I'm feeling under the weather, I love a slice of bread, buttered and covered with honey! I enjoy it! So is God's word to give us delight (Psalm 1:2; Ezekiel 3:3).

Lord, Thy Word abideth,
And our footsteps guideth;
Who its truth believeth
Light and joy receiveth.

When our foes are near us,
Then Thy Word doth cheer us,
Word of consolation,
Message of salvation.

When the storms are o'er us,
And dark clouds before us,
Then its light directeth,
And our way protecteth.

Who can tell the pleasure,
Who recount the treasure,
By Thy Word imparted,
To the simple-hearted?

Word of mercy, giving
Succour to the living;
Word of life, supplying
Comfort to the dying!

O that we, discerning
Its most holy learning,
Lord, may love and fear Thee,
Evermore be near Thee!

Henry Williams Baker, 1821–77

Conclusion

It is good to have a daily 'quiet time': an opportunity every day to give God time to speak into our lives as we meditate on his word and pray.

'As the rain and the snow come down from heaven, and do not return to it without watering the earth and making it bud and flourish . . ., so is my word that goes out from my mouth. It will not return to me empty, but will accomplish what I desire and achieve the purpose for which I sent it' (Isaiah 55:10–11).

2

PROMISES IN PRAYER

Key thought The amazing Bible promises about prayer are intended to be an incentive for us to be honest with God, taking him at his word in the here and now of our lives.

Key Bible verse 'Ask and it will be given to you; seek and you will find; knock and the door will be opened to you. For everyone who asks receives; he who seeks finds; and to him who knocks, the door will be opened' (Jesus, in Matthew 7:7-8).

Promises in prayer: Matthew 7:7-11

'Help,' I cried. And that, in a word, is prayer. But the problem is not that we don't know that prayer works – that it changes things, that it changes us, that it changes circumstances. The problem is actually doing it and keeping at it – keeping praying to our Lord and Saviour.

These verses are a great stimulus to prayer, if ever we needed it. They promise answers: '. . . it *will* be given to you . . . you *will* find . . . the door *will* be opened to you . . . for *everyone* . . .' Wow! These really are *some* words! As Dr Martyn Lloyd-Jones comments, 'I cannot imagine a better, more cheering or a more comforting statement with which to face all the uncertainties and hazards of our life in this world of time than that contained in verses 7–11. It is one of those great comprehensive and gracious promises which are to be found only in the Bible. There is nothing that can be more encouraging as we face life with all its uncertainties and possibilities, our "future all unknown".'

Here are some further New Testament promises in prayer:

- 'I tell you that if two of you on earth agree about anything you ask for, it will be done for you by my Father in heaven' (Matthew 18:19).

- 'If you believe, you will receive whatever you ask for in prayer' (Matthew 21:22).

- 'Whatever you ask for in prayer, believe that you have received it, and it will be yours' (Mark 11:24).

- 'And I will do whatever you ask in my name, so that the Son may bring glory to the Father. You may ask me for anything in my name, and I will do it' (John 14:13–14).

- 'If you remain in me, and my words remain in you, ask whatever you wish, and it will be given you' (John 15:7).

- 'In that day you will no longer ask me anything. I tell you the truth, my Father will give you whatever you ask in my name. Until now you have not asked for anything in my name. Ask and you will receive, and your joy will be complete' (John 16:23–24).

- '[We] receive from him anything we ask, because we obey his commands and do what pleases him' (1 John 3:22).

- 'This is the confidence we have in approaching God: that if we ask anything according to his will, he hears us' (1 John 5:14).

Scripture points to certain hindrances that may block our prayers:

- Sin that remains unconfessed (Psalm 66:18).

- Wrong motives (James 4:3).

- Not taking God at his word (Matthew 13:53–58); double-mindedness (James 1:5–7).

- Cherishing unforgiveness (Mark 11:25–26).

- Wrong relationships (Matthew 5:23–24).

- Vain repetition (Matthew 6:7).

These following questions may be helpful as we think about our own life with God.

- Do we constantly realize our need of God – or as we get older and more 'mature' (so we think) as Christians do we think that we don't need God's help as much as we did when we were younger in the faith?

- Do we regularly quieten our spirits as we come to pray? How can we be encouraged to remember that God is our Father and that we're adopted into his family?

- How honest are we when we pray? For example, if in our hearts we aren't sure that it is God's will for a particular person to be healed how do we pray on that occasion?

- What are you asking God for at this time in your life? Are you managing to keep on praying? If you're finding the going tough, how can others help you in your prayers?

'The possibilities of prayer run parallel with the promises of God,' wrote E. M. Bounds. What, then, are some of the certainties that we can ask God for?

- The gospel *will* reach to the ends of the earth (Matthew 24:14). How about praying for your own witness, and the witness of 'ordinary' Christians, the preaching of God's word in your own country and throughout the world, and the conversion of non-Christian friends and relatives?

- God's word *will* have an effect on those who hear it (Isaiah 55:10–11). How about praying for the one who will speak to you this Sunday at church: his preparation, that he will be close to God, that he will know God speaking to him first and that the message will come home powerfully to all the listeners, that God's word will be explained and unleashed throughout the world, and that we will all be obedient to put that word into practice.

Finally, here are some more encouragements to pray:

- 'The prayer of a righteous man is powerful and effective' (James 5:16).

- 'It is because God has promised certain things that we can ask for them with the full assurance of faith' (A. W. Pink).

- 'Prayer is not wrestling with God's reluctance to bless us; it is laying hold of his willingness to do so' (John Blanchard).

- 'Satan is not afraid of prayerless study, prayerless work or prayerless religion . . . but he will tremble when we pray' (Samuel Chadwick).

> What a Friend we have in Jesus,
>   All our sins and griefs to bear!
> What a privilege to carry
>   Everything to God in prayer!
> O what peace we often forfeit,
>   O what needless pain we bear,
> All because we do not carry
>   Everything to God in prayer!
>
> Have we trials and temptations?
>   Is there trouble anywhere?
> We should never be discouraged:

Take it to the Lord in prayer.
Can we find a friend so faithful,
  Who will all our sorrows share?
Jesus knows our every weakness:
  Take it to the Lord in prayer.

Are we weak and heavy-laden,
  Cumbered with a load of care?
Precious Saviour, still our refuge:
  Take it to the Lord in prayer.
Do thy friends despise, forsake thee?
  Take it to the Lord in prayer;
In His arms He'll take and shield thee,
  Thou wilt find a solace there.

Joseph Medlicott Scriven, 1819–86

Conclusion
Prayer isn't a technique, 'twisting God's arm' to fit in
with our purposes. When we pray, we submit our wills
to God. It is by prayer that we find out what God's
will is, we take hold of it, and we live according to it.

'If you remain in me and my words remain in you,
ask whatever you wish, and it will be given you' (Jesus,
in John 15:7).

THE PROMISE OF STRENGTH

Key thought Every day of our lives we need God's strength to equip us.

Key Bible verse 'Your strength will equal your days' (Deuteronomy 33:25).

The secret of strength

'When we come to many of the promises of God we find ourselves embarrassed with spiritual riches. There seems to be so much land to possess. This is particularly true when dealing with promises related to *strength* and *power* . . . there are over 700 references to this possession' (Herbert Lockyer). Read through just a few of them:

- 'The LORD is my strength and my song; he has become my salvation' (Exodus 15:2).
- 'Look to the LORD and his strength; seek his face always' (1 Chronicles 16:11).
- 'The LORD is my strength and my shield; my heart trusts in him, and I am helped. My heart leaps for joy and I will give thanks to him in song' (Psalm 28:7).
- 'You, O God, are strong . . . you, O Lord, are loving' (Psalm 62:11).
- 'Surely God is my salvation; I will trust and not be afraid. The LORD, the LORD, is my strength and my song' (Isaiah 12:2).
- 'Those who hope in the LORD will renew their strength' (Isaiah 40:31).

- 'The Sovereign LORD is my strength; he makes my feet like the feet of a deer, he enables me to go on the heights' (Habakkuk 3:19).
- 'I can do everything through him who gives me strength' (Philippians 4:13).

Of ourselves we are weak, and the more we are aware of our weakness the better, because then God can show his power (Joel 3:10; 2 Corinthians 12:7–10). Apart from him, we have no strength against our enemies, no wisdom, no power to face difficulties.

'As thy days, so shall thy strength be'

The words in this heading are from the Authorized (King James) Version; in the NIV this verse read, 'Your strength will equal your days' (Deuteronomy 33:25). Don't we find this to be true? We are given strength for each day. We may sit and wonder if we have enough strength for tomorrow or next year or ten years' time. But God promises us sufficient resources – himself – for the present day. Strength won't be given *before* we need it, but given just *when* we need it.

- *In times of crisis.* Being a Christian does not guarantee us immunity from life's trials, sorrows, and sufferings. At times when something earth-shattering happens – when the bottom falls out of our world – we need God's strength. We need to know that he is with us 'even though [we] walk through the valley of the shadow of death'. In times of major personal disaster, we may know God's deliverance (Psalm 37:39–40), but at other times it may be God's will for us to know his presence, his companionship, in the midst of difficulty and danger (Psalm 23:4).

- *In times of temptation.* Temptation isn't sin, but it is nevertheless real. We need God's strength and help to deal with the temptations that come to us. We need to remember that because Jesus himself was tempted, he can help us (Hebrews 2:18; 4:15–16). We need to remember that with Christ's help we *are* more than conquerors (Romans 8:37). We need to see the way out from temptation that he provides (1 Corinthians 10:13). *We* act with God (Psalm 141:3), remembering that we have been made new people (Romans 6:1–11). Things have become different now that we are Christians! Sin is no longer the controlling factor in our lives. That old relationship with sin is over and done with; our new master – God himself – is the only one who has a legitimate claim on us; so our lives are to be lived to please him (Romans 6:12–14).

But what happens when, as believers, we sin? Does God give up on us? No! Look up Job 22:23: 'If you return to the Almighty, you will be restored.' With repentance and faith we need to turn away from sin, whether they are 'big' or 'little' sins in our eyes. God will mend the mess we have made of our lives – if we return to him.

• *In ordinary times.* How do we keep going in the plain, ordinary (and at times, let's say it, monotonous) days of life, when things just keep ticking along more or less nicely? How do we cope at work, at home, at college? We are to derive our strength from God. We're to remember that ultimately we're not working for our boss, but for God (Colossians 3:22–25). Wherever we are, we're to live all our lives in submission to God. The parallel passage to the one just mentioned ends with 'Finally, be strong in the Lord and in his mighty power' (Ephesians 6:1–10), before going into the verses that describe the armour of God. We need God's strength for the ordinary everydays of our lives!

And how?

How do we become strong, then? By performing some special 'spiritual gymnastics'? Well, no, not exactly! The foundation of our strength is the gospel, the means by which the power of God comes to work in us (Romans 1:16; 1 Corinthians 1:18). As believers, we're to submit ourselves to God (James 4:7–8). This means coming to him in faith (1 John 5:4–5), in an attitude not of unbelief (Romans 4:20), but of quietness and trust (Psalm 27:14; Isaiah 30:15). Our inner strength derives from God, his joy (Nehemiah 8:10; Isaiah 12:2–3) and his power (Ephesians 3:16; 6:10; Colossians 1:11) – his power that raised Jesus from the dead (Ephesians 1:19–20). We will want to be strong in his word (Colossians 3:16; 2 Timothy 3:16–17; end of 1 John 2:14), then. And of course becoming strong is something gradual: we're to keep on growing stronger and stronger!

There are some lovely words in 2 Samuel 23:16: 'Jonathan went to David . . . and helped him to find strength in God.' Sometimes we can't get by on our own. We need others' help; we need others who will encourage us to look to God when we're really down. Is there someone now who is near to you whom you could help in such a way?

Give me strength!

Do you get afraid at times? I do. We need to remember God's words: 'Say to those with fearful hearts, "Be strong, do not fear; your God will come" ' (Isaiah 35:4), '[I will] save you . . . Do not be afraid, but let your hands be strong' (Zechariah 8:13). I like such verses, because they're honest: they recognize the reality of fear while at the same time showing God's answer – himself. 'For God did not give us a spirit of timidity [AV, 'fear'], but a spirit of power, of love and of self-discipline' (2 Timothy 1:7).

Our response

What are God's strong people to do, then? Just sit around twiddling their super-sized spiritual thumbs? Er, no. 'The people that . . . know their God shall be strong, and do

exploits' (Daniel 11:32, Authorized (King James) Version).
Do we not need more strong Christians who will perform
great acts for God? Do we not need more courageous
believers (1 Corinthians 16:13), on fire with a love for God
(Psalm 18:1; Mark 12:30); zealous in encouraging other
believers (Acts 18:23; 1 Thessalonians 3:2), and being the
salt and light in a rotting, dark, and needy world (Matthew
5:13–16; 28:18–20; Luke 10:25–37)?

'We rest on Thee', our Shield and our Defender!
　　We go not forth alone against the foe;
Strong in Thy strength, safe in Thy keeping tender,
　　'We rest on Thee, and in Thy Name we go.'

Yes, 'in Thy Name', O Captain of salvation!
　　In Thy dear Name, all other names above;
Jesus our Righteousness, our sure Foundation,
　　Our Prince of glory and our King of love.

'We go' in faith, our own great weakness feeling,
　　And needing more each day Thy grace to know;
Yet from our hearts a song of triumph pealing:
　　'We rest on Thee, and in Thy Name we go.'

'We rest on Thee', our Shield and our Defender!
　　Thine is the battle; Thine shall be the praise
When passing through the gates of pearly splendour,
　　Victors, we rest with Thee through endless days.

　　　　　　　　　Edith Adeline Gilling Cherry 1872–97

Conclusion

'God's strength reinforces the fragile abilities of man.
This enables him to do great exploits for God' (Wayne
Detzler).

'The LORD is my strength and my song; he has become
my salvation' (Exodus 15:2).

4

THE PROMISE OF COMFORT

Key thought None of us gets through life without meeting trouble or sorrow at some time, but we can still experience the comfort and love of God in our difficulties.

Key Bible verse 'The God of all comfort, who comforts us in all our troubles' (2 Corinthians 1:3–4).

The source of comfort

There is no other book of comfort in the whole world that is comparable to the Bible. Because God is 'the God of all comfort' (2 Corinthians 1:3–4), we expect to find his word full of comfort and we are certainly not disappointed, as these few instances show:

- 'You, O LORD, have helped me and comforted me' (Psalm 86:17).
- 'May your unfailing love be my comfort, according to your promise to your servant' (Psalm 119:76).
- 'Comfort, comfort my people, says your God. Speak tenderly to Jerusalem . . .' (Isaiah 40:1–2).
- 'Shout for joy, O heavens; rejoice, O earth; burst into song, O mountains! For the LORD comforts his people and will have compassion on his afflicted ones' (Isaiah 49:13).
- 'I will turn their mourning into gladness; I will give them comfort and joy instead of sorrow' (Jeremiah 31:13).

Promises of comfort

Promises of comfort in the Bible are associated with help and encouragement in times of stress, sorrow, and difficulty. They show that God is deeply interested in all that goes on in our lives. Here is a list of Bible verses and other references that show us God's help at different times of our Christian lives. You could read and think about these when:

● afraid.

  □ 'I sought the LORD, and he answered me; he delivered me from all my fears' (Psalm 34:4).

  □ See also Psalm 27; 46; 56; 91; Matthew 8:23–27.

● anxious or worried.

  □ 'Cast all your anxiety on him because he cares for you' (1 Peter 5:7).

  □ See also Isaiah 43:1–13; Matthew 6:25–34; 11:28; Philippians 4:4–7.

● bereaved.

  □ 'Blessed are those who mourn, for they will be comforted' (Matthew 5:4).

  □ See also Psalm 23; John 11:21–27; 1 Corinthians 15:51–57; 1 Thessalonians 4:13–18; Revelation 21:1–5.

● discouraged.

  □ 'Why are you downcast, O my soul? Why so disturbed within me? Put your hope in God' (Psalm 42:5).

  □ See also Psalm 34:18; 40:1–3; Lamentations 3:20–23; Romans 8:28–39; 2 Corinthians 4:7–18.

● failure and sin come.

  □ 'But God demonstrates his own love for us in this. While we were still sinners, Christ died for us' (Romans 5:8).

  □ See also Psalm 51: Luke 15:11–24.

● far from God.

  □ 'My Father, who has given them to me, is greater

than all; no-one can snatch them out of my Father's hand' (John 10:29).

☐ See also Psalm 139:1–18; Acts 17:24–31; James 4:8.

● ill or in pain.

☐ 'My grace is sufficient for you, for my power is made perfect in weakness' (2 Corinthians 12:9).

☐ See also Psalm 103:1–4; Romans 8:18–25; 2 Corinthians 4:16–18.

● lonely.

☐ 'So do not fear, for I am with you; do not be dismayed, for I am your God' (Isaiah 41:10).

☐ See also Psalm 73:23–24; Isaiah 49:14–16; John 14:15–21.

● needing peace.

☐ 'You will keep in perfect peace him whose mind is steadfast, because he trusts in you' (Isaiah 26:3).

☐ See also John 14:27; Romans 5:1–5; Philippians 4:4–7.

● tired.

☐ 'Come to me, all you who are weary and burdened, and I will give you rest. Take my yoke upon you and learn from me, for I am gentle and humble in heart, and you will find rest for your souls. For my yoke is easy and my burden is light' (Matthew 11:28–30).

☐ See also Isaiah 40:28–31; 2 Corinthians 4:16–18.

● weak.

☐ 'For we do not have a high priest who is unable to sympathise with our weaknesses, but we have one who has been tempted in every way, just as we are – yet was without sin. Let us then approach the throne of grace with confidence, so that we may receive mercy and find grace to help us in our time of need' (Hebrews 4:15–16).

☐ See also Joshua 1:6–9; 2 Corinthians 12:9–10; Philippians 4:12–13.

The experience of comfort

None of us gets through life without meeting trouble and
sorrow at some time (Job 5:7). We wonder where God is;
we don't feel him near us. What do we do? We can tell
God our troubles, knowing that he understands. He is
certainly with us, even if he seems to us to be remote. You
may find some of the verses given above helpful in coming
near to him.

The basic problem is that we live in a fallen world, one
originally made good but spoilt dreadfully by sin. And we
are by nature fallen, sinful human beings. The Christian
message is one of comfort *in* trouble (Psalm 9:9; 46:1),
and at times deliverance *from* trouble (e.g. Psalm 50:15;
Proverbs 12:21). Our confidence is in the God who acted
in history, identifying himself with us fully, and dealing
with our sin and its consequences in the sacrifice of his Son
(Isaiah 53:3–12).

As Christians we are to rest secure in the big issue of
life – our standing before God (Romans 5:1–4). He has
given us his Spirit, the Comforter or Counsellor (John
14:18), to live within us. The Spirit brings us to know that
Jesus and the Father love us dearly (John 15:15–21). We
can be secure in God and his love (Deuteronomy 33:27),
not in our meagre strength.

Do you believe in angels? God's spiritual messengers,
'God's secret agents' as Billy Graham calls them. They
are real! They are the friends of believers, defending and
delivering them (e.g. Psalm 34:7; 91:11–12; Daniel 6:22;
Acts 5:19; Hebrews 1:14).

Why?

Why do we go through problems? Ultimately 'the mystery
of why a particular individual suffers as he or she does
remains shrouded and hidden' (Lawrence O. Richards).
Without wanting to give easy, slick reasons, suffering is

sometimes allowed by God as a punishment for sin (Job 4:7–9) or as discipline (Hebrews 12:5–13). It may well lead to a deeper trust (Job 42:1–6), strengthen our character (Psalm 119:67, 71; Romans 5:3–4) and be to God's glory (John 9:1–7).

There are special promises of blessing for those who suffer for righteousness' sake (Matthew 5:10–12; 1 Peter 3:14–18).

Pass it on

Sometimes we go through problems, 'come out the other side', and find later that we can help those who are meeting with the same difficulties (2 Corinthians 1:4). We can share our first-hand experience of God's comfort and help.

How firm a foundation, ye saints of the Lord,
Is laid for your faith in His excellent Word!
What more can He say than to you He has said –
You, who unto Jesus for refuge have fled?

In every condition – in sickness, in health,
In poverty's vale, or abounding in wealth;
At home or abroad, on the land, on the sea,
As days may demand, shall thy strength ever be.

Fear not, I am with thee, O be not dismayed!
I, I am thy God, and will still give thee aid:
I'll strengthen thee, help thee, and cause thee to stand,
Upheld by My righteous, omnipotent hand.

When through the deep waters I cause thee to go,
The rivers of woe shall not thee overflow;
For I will be with thee, thy troubles to bless,
And sanctify to thee thy deepest distress.

When through fiery trials thy pathway shall lie,
My grace all-sufficient shall be thy supply;

The flame shall not hurt thee: I only design
Thy dross to consume, and thy gold to refine.

The soul that on Jesus has leaned for repose
I will not, I will not desert to its foes;
That soul, though all hell should endeavour to shake,
I'll never, no never, no never forsake!

'K' in Rippon's Selection, 1787

Conclusion

God is the sure foundation of our Christian lives. He
never stops looking after us, even when we don't feel
he is near. Absolutely nothing can cut us off from him
and his love!

'I am convinced that neither death nor life, neither
angels nor demons, neither the present nor the future,
nor any powers, neither height nor depth, nor anything else in all creation, will be able to separate us
from the love of God that is in Christ Jesus our Lord'
(Romans 8:38–39).

5

THE PROMISE OF JOY

> *Key thought* The source of the Christian's joy is in God himself.
>
> *Key Bible verse* 'The joy of the LORD is your strength' (Nehemiah 8:10).

The joy of knowing God

As Christians we can really know joy. Our sins are forgiven, we are declared to be in a right relationship with God and we are his children. The way into his presence is open! Real joy follows coming to believe in the Lord Jesus Christ (Acts 8:39; 16:34; Romans 5:11; 1 Peter 1:6, 8).

We have fellowship with God; we know God himself: 'You have made known to me the path of life; you will fill me with joy in your presence' (Psalm 16:11). Such a joy is experienced when believers come together (Isaiah 35:10), and remains even in times of trouble (Habakkuk 3:17–18).

Our God wants us to enjoy life (John 10:10). He has given us so much. While recognizing that his gifts can be abused, we know that he wants us to accept and enjoy all the good things he has given us in a spirit of contentment and thankfulness (1 Timothy 6:6, 17). This of course applies to what we narrowly call 'spiritual' but it also surely applies to the mundane stuff of life – the ordinary tasks such as our daily work and household chores such as the washing-up!

The Bible also links joy with suffering and persecution.

The response of the first Christians to persecution and suffering was an inner certain joy that was independent of circumstances (Acts 13:49–52; 2 Corinthians 6:10; 7:4; James 1:2–3; 1 Peter 1:6–9). Again, we see the utter realism of the Bible. Christians aren't exempt from difficulties, but there can be joy even through tears.

And beyond this present world, there is a complete joy that will last for ever. It will never fail. All tears and death will be no more and we will be with God for ever, caught up in glory, in worship and adoration of 'him that sits on the throne and the Lamb' (Romans 5:2; Revelation 5; 21:1–4).

What is joy?

Joy can't really be put into words (1 Peter 1:8). We can, however, describe it in some ways. It isn't passing, super-ficial or artificial happiness. It's perhaps more a quality of life than an emotion. It's a deep, constant sense of well-being with God. It comes from God!

- *Joy comes from the Holy Spirit.* 'The disciples were filled with joy and with the Holy Spirit' (Acts 13:52). Joy is a part of the fruit of the Spirit (Galatians 5:22). It is recorded of Jesus that he was 'full of joy through the Holy Spirit' (Luke 10:21). See also Romans 14:17; Ephesians 5:18–20; 1 Thessalonians 1:6.

- *Joy comes from the Lord Jesus Christ.* As we stay close to Jesus, constantly acknowledging our dependence on him, we will know his joy (John 15:1–11). There are special promises of joy in two areas:
  □ When we do what Jesus wants us to do, when we obey him, we will know the fulfilment of the promise of his joy (John 15:10–11).
  □ When we pray, we will receive answers to our prayers and know complete joy (John 16:24).

  Paul tells the Philippians to 'rejoice in the Lord

always' (Philippians 4:4). Given the difficulty of constantly rejoicing in our Saviour (not our circumstances), he adds 'I will say it again: Rejoice!'

● *Joy comes from God the Father.* Nehemiah encouraged the people, 'The joy of the LORD is your strength' (Nehemiah 8:10). Joy derived from God would make them – and indeed makes us – strong.

Experiencing joy

The Puritan minister and writer Thomas Watson (died about 1686) noted, 'There are two things that I have always looked upon as difficult. The one is, to make the wicked sad: the other is to make the godly joyful.' He was right: most of us lack the overflowing joy of God that is ours by rights.

Why is this? And what can we do about it? Let's be constructive rather than condemning!

● *Stop and think!* Most of us fail to grasp the truths of the faith and to reflect on them. We're content with the superficial. We fail to think long and hard about what God has done in us and for us. If we did, then the amazing fact of our salvation would surely grip us and lead us to rejoice in God. Look again at the joy on the resurrection morning (Matthew 28:1–10)!

● *Pray and praise!* Let's meditate on the Scriptures, and let them be a source of joy and delight to us (Psalm 1:2; 19:8; 119:14, 162). The Bible tells us about God, his world, and us. It's only as we let our minds sink deep into it, as we allow Christ's words to abide in us (John 15:3, 7), that we will know joy. Truth is the basis of experience. And we may well need more sensitive, open hearts – not a stubborn 'I know it all already' attitude. Notice, too, that Paul's command to rejoice comes in the context of prayer (Philippians 4:4–7).

Joy in the Bible isn't just something we experience by

ourselves; it's seen as the believing community of God gathers to worship and praise God. The psalmist looks back: 'How I used to go with the multitude, leading the procession to the house of God, with shouts of joy and thanksgiving among the festive throng' (Psalm 42:4). Read David's song of thanks (1 Chronicles 16:8–36) after the ark has been brought to Jerusalem; read Psalms 95 and 100, and see if you aren't moved at these acts of corporate worship!

Is the Sabbath a delight to us – do we *enjoy* Sundays (Isaiah 58:13)? Do we *enjoy* praying? Do we *enjoy* God? Or has our Christian life become something of a drag?

• *Share and encourage!* The reality of Christian fellowship bursts out from the pages of the New Testament: 'All the believers were together and had everything in common' (Acts 2:44). 'Everyone has heard about your obedience, so I am full of joy over you' (Romans 16:19). 'In all my prayers for all of you, I always pray with joy because of your partnership in the gospel from the first day until now' (Philippians 1:4). 'How can we thank God enough for you in return for all the joy we have in the presence of our God because of you?' (1 Thessalonians 3:9). 'Recalling your tears, I long to see you, so that I may be filled with joy' (2 Timothy 1:4). 'I have no greater joy than to hear that my children are walking in the truth' (3 John 4). What warmth there was amongst these believers! We will need to translate these principles into our own culture, but surely we've got a long way to go! When was the last time you or I had a good encouraging conversation with someone on Christian things? We find it easier to talk about football, the weather, the service that we've just been joining in, but how often do we share our own appreciation of God?

> Come, we that love the Lord,
> And let our joys be known;

Join in a song with sweet accord,
   And thus surround the throne.

The sorrows of the mind
   Be banished from the place;
Religion never was designed
   To make our pleasures less.

Let those refuse to sing
   That never knew our God;
But children of the heavenly King
   May speak their joys abroad.

The God who rules on high,
   And thunders if He please,
Who rides upon the stormy sky
   And manages the seas –

This aweful God is ours,
   Our Father and our love;
He will send down His heavenly powers
   To carry us above.

The men of grace have found
   Glory begun below;
Celestial fruit on earthly ground
   From faith and hope may grow.

The hill of Zion yields
   A thousand sacred sweets,
Before we reach the heavenly fields,
   Or walk the golden streets.

Then let our songs abound,
   And every tear be dry;
We're marching through Immanuel's ground
   To fairer worlds on high.

Isaac Watts, 1674–1748

Conclusion

Hallelujah! Isn't God great! Let's celebrate his goodness and make him known in the world of today!

'I delight greatly in the LORD; my soul rejoices in my God. For he has clothed me with garments of salvation and arrayed me in a robe of righteousness' (Isaiah 61:10).

6

THE PROMISE OF GUIDANCE

Key thought We can be confident that God's promises to guide us *will* be fulfilled.

Key Bible verse Trust in the LORD with all your heart and lean not on your own understanding; in all your ways acknowledge him, and he will make your paths straight' (Proverbs 3:5–6).

Guidance: 'the bottom line'

Let's be honest: guidance is a problem. How do I know which job to take? Which person to marry? Where to live? Which courses to study?

Bob Horn recalls attending a student conference: 'We all came expecting advice on practical problems: how to know God's will, how to choose between different jobs, how to be sure our motives are pure, what if we miss God's way? The speaker began. He talked about the character of God and seemed a long time getting to the subject. He expounded on God as the Covenant God, the great Shepherd of His flock. He continued about His unlimited power and sovereign purposes. Then he stopped. It was all over and we felt cheated. We had come for practical help, not preaching or a theological discourse.

'In fact we had been given the most practical help possible. On reflection we began to see that this actually solved the greatest problem about guidance. Like others, we had had two worries about this question: first, whether God could or would guide us at all; and secondly, how we should know what that guidance (if any) was. The second worry assumes enormous proportions if we are uncertain about the first; but justification [being considered right with God] settles the first. God is God and He is for us. He is not a celestial careers bureau, able to help only when we ring Him up. Our whole life is in His hands. We do not have to persuade Him to guide. He has been guiding, every minute – as our justification proves. He is guiding right now. He will guide all through. "Your God is King, your Father reigns."

'We do not have to ask God to step in. He is in already. We need rather to ask for discernment to grasp His will and grace to do it' (*Go Free!* IVP).

Before we go any further, let's remember these 'bottom-line' facts: as believers, we are put into a right relationship with God. This is the crucial fact in guidance. God *is* already with us; he knows us and we know him.

Ways of guidance

How does God guide us? Here are some 'strands'; when all the strands are woven together, our conviction about some particular guidance will be strong. If only one strand is present, it is probably wise to wait for additional confirmation. God guides us:

● *through the Bible.* 'Your word is a lamp to my feet and a light for my path' (Psalm 119:105). But how do we use the Bible in guidance? We aren't just to open it up at a random page, picking out the first verse that looks suitable. No, as we 'let the word of Christ dwell in [us] richly' (Colossians 3:16), then we will know God's mind on the issues that face us. As we regularly have God's input into our lives through his word (reading by ourselves, hearing sermons, discussing it with others), so we will see biblical principles at work (Romans 12:2).

The basic guidance God gives us is to shape our lives,

to instil in us fundamental attitudes, ideals, understandings. These come through a constant exposure to the
Bible. Gradually we will come to have 'God's mind', as
God's word affects our consciences, our wills, our brains.
So God's guidance fundamentally is expressed as positive
guidelines for living. 'Work out your responsibilities as
a husband, wife, to your children', 'Be the type of man/
woman/child God wants you to be', and so on. We know
that it is *always* God's will for us to be such people. (See,
e.g., Paul's commands in Romans 8:13–14 – putting sins
to death is part of being led by the Spirit; Colossians
3:5—4:1; 1 Peter 1:16.)

Sometimes, to be sure, a passage will jump out at us
from the page of the Bible. This is all well and good
but such verses 'will seldom constitute clear guidance
without further confirmation' (David Watson, *One in the
Spirit*).

• *through our circumstances*. Circumstances are very important in guidance. By circumstances I include our existing
commitments or obligations. If we are in the middle of
a three-year course at college, it is highly unlikely that
it is God's will that we should suddenly leave, even to
go and be a missionary in some far-flung land. (Our
guidance on such an issue may be little more than wish-
ful thinking expressed in a spiritual – or super-spiritual
– manner.)

Sometimes the way before us is 'blocked'. 'No doors
open' for us, as we put it. This happened to Paul and
his companions (Acts 16:6–7). At other times, openings
suddenly come out of the blue. Philip's guidance (Acts
8:26) was certainly unexpected.

You see, we are meant to use our minds, to think
about circumstances and about the kind of people we
are. We may expect extraordinary special revelations
from God, whereas God wants us to use our minds, to
think, to plan, to see the long-term outcome of our plans.

(Remember 'love . . . God . . . with all your mind', Matthew 22:37?) We may think it's unspiritual to use our minds, whereas in fact the reverse is true, it's unspiritual not to! We're not like senseless mules, after all (Psalm 32:8–9)!

To be sure, we do make mistakes; we sin; we ignore God; we go against his directions. Is everything lost? Is the damage irrevocable? No! Do we really believe Romans 8:28: '. . . in all things God works for the good of those who love him'? God not only makes up for our waywardness; he also somehow takes our mistakes into his plan for us and brings good from them.

- *through other Christians*. Here we are sometimes too proud to ask others' help. We may *tell* our Christian friends, 'This is what I'm doing.' Or we may ask for their advice when we know they'll agree with us! How serious are we about genuinely informing our circle of Christian friends about a particular need? And are we really prepared to listen to their guiding words? Often, others are better judges of our own characters and gifts than we are ourselves. 'A wise man listens to advice' (Proverbs 12:15). It's not unspiritual or immature to ask for others' help, advice, and prayers. Friends are honest (Proverbs 27:6). And even the apostle Paul asked others to pray for him (Romans 15:31–32; Ephesians 6:19). How 'open to reason' are we (James 3:17, RSV; 'submissive', NIV)?

- *through prayer*. We certainly need a sense of peace in our hearts, alongside other strands of guidance, as we commit our life to God (Psalm 37:3–5). 'It seemed good to the Holy Spirit and to us' (Acts 15:28) shows a good balance between the objective and the subjective. The peace of Christ is to act as a ruler, an umpire, an arbiter in our lives (Colossians 3:15). As Christians we often, but not always, have a sense of peace when we come to a right decision. How do we come to such a peace? By quietly waiting upon God. This takes time. The other month I had an issue that I needed God to settle. The matter had been dragging on for a little while and other people were pushing me for a decision. I prayed regularly about the matter; and I set aside some time on a Saturday morning to wait on God. I went out into the country in the car. It took me a long time to become still before God. It took me a long time to repent of certain matters – and then to my mind came a Scripture verse quietly which was God's word to me. God does guide us by his Spirit as we wait on him in prayer. Look through Acts, for example: Acts 8:29; 10:19; 13:2; 16:6–7.

Note that such 'direct words' must always be within the limits of the Bible. We all know of people who claim God has spoken to them about this and that, which turns out to be something outlandish and/or foolish!

The Spirit emphatically does not lead us to consider the absolutes of Scripture just as historically and culturally relative matters that we can either take or leave. We cannot say that a certain word, for example on marrying an unbeliever or running off with someone else's wife, does not apply to us in a certain instance. Guidance on such issues is as plain as a pikestaff in God's word.

Decisions, decisions

At the end of the day, we need to make a decision. If at all possible, we need to *wait* until we are sure before God that a particular course of action is right. In these days of instant everything, we want instant guidance from God. (Odd isn't it, how we want instant guidance but aren't really prepared for instant obedience!) Often we will need to wait upon God for an answer. We then need to take a decision and trust God that this is the right one. We do this by leaving him to take us on to the next stage; by not worrying about the decision we've made and by not going back on it.

Knowing the way

It is important to remember that guidance is only one part of our Christian lives. We aren't just to pray when we want to know God's will on a certain matter. 'In all your ways acknowledge him, and he will make your paths straight' (Proverbs 3:6). We are to try to keep a close relationship with God and serve him all the time. Notice, for example, the promise of guidance (verse 11) in a section about a lifestyle of serving others in true righteousness (Isaiah 58:6–14). Guidance is part of the believer's lifestyle. God goes before us (Deuteronomy 31:8).

> Be still, my soul: the Lord is on thy side;
>   Bear patiently the cross of grief or pain;
> Leave to thy God to order and provide;
>   In every change He faithful will remain.
> Be still, my soul: thy best, thy heavenly Friend
> Through thorny ways leads to a joyful end.
>
> Be still, my soul; thy God doth undertake
>   To guide the future as He has the past.
> Thy hope, thy confidence, let nothing shake;
>   All now mysterious shall be bright at last.
> Be still, my soul: the waves and winds still know
> His voice who ruled them while He dwelt below.
>
> Be still, my soul: the hour is hastening on
>   When we shall be for ever with the Lord,
> When disappointment, grief and fear are gone,
>   Sorrow forgot, love's purest joys restored.
> Be still, my soul: when change and tears are past,
> All safe and blessed we shall meet at last.
>
>   Katharina von Schlegel, born 1697
>   tr. by Jane Laurie Borthwick, 1813–97

Conclusion

God is not reluctant to show us the pattern he wants for our lives. After all, he has already given us so much! We may not always be able to see his way, but he is certainly guiding us in it.

'I will instruct you and teach you in the way you should go; I will counsel you and watch over you' (Psalm 32:8).

7

THROUGH ALL THE CHANGING SCENES OF LIFE

Key thought Even though the situations we find ourselves in change through our lives, we can always
know that God is with us, providing for our needs.

Key Bible verse 'Godliness with contentment is great
gain. For we brought nothing into the world, and we
can take nothing out of it. But if we have food and
clothing, we will be content with that' (1 Timothy
6:6–8).

Our needs

When it comes down to it, what do we need in life? I've
just spent the past weekend clearing out some cupboards
and fairly easily managed to throw out four dustbins full.
We do clutter up our lives with a lot of things we don't
really need!

Let's look at some of the essentials of life and what God
says about the following different basics:

- Food. This is given to us by God (Psalm 111:5; Matthew
  6:11, 25–33). Should we not be more thankful, and less
  anxious? And should we not continue to care for those
  in our world without sufficient food?

- Clothes. Again these come from God (Matthew
  6:25–33); so our anxieties can be removed. Surely Jesus
  must have been suitably clothed as he moved around;
  he would not have been carelessly dressed. On the other

hand it would be wrong to make 'idols' out of clothes. Our health and holiness are more important than our garments; the spiritual is more important than the physical.

- Money and possessions. Many of us spend a lot of time thinking about how we can get more money. But this is a sign that we are serving money, not God. And it's just impossible to serve both (Matthew 6:24). We know the power of the love of money (1 Timothy 6:10) and our possessions (Luke 12:15–21). The money and possessions we have aren't in fact really ours; they're God's. We are to be good stewards of them – looking after them carefully. How does this work out in practice?

  ☐ God will give us what we need (Psalm 34:9–10; 37:25; Philippians 4:19). This may mean buying second-hand clothes or goods rather than new ones. There are some fine goodies to be had in Oxfam shops!

  ☐ We should use the money we have wisely. We need to take care of our families. We need to be generous in our giving – and happy too. (The word 'cheerful' in 'God loves a cheerful giver', 2 Corinthians 9:7, is *hilarios*, from which we get our word 'hilarious'.) A giving of one-tenth (but not in a legalistic or showy manner!) would seem appropriate (Malachi 3:10; Matthew 6:1–4; Luke 18:12).

  ☐ We can use our time and home generously, for example by being hospitable and inviting others to our home to read the Bible.

  You see, many of us are fairly comfortably off – certainly better off than those of one, two, or three generations ago. Yet are we content? 'Godliness with contentment is great gain. For we brought nothing into the world, and we can take nothing out of it. But if we have food and clothing, we will be content with that' (1 Timothy 6:6–8). 'I know what it is to have plenty. I have learned the secret of being content in any and every situation, whether well fed or hungry, whether living in plenty or in want. I can do everything through him who gives me strength' (Philippians 4:12–13). Have we learnt this secret of remaining 'calm in adversity, humble in prosperity', as William Hendriksen puts it? Or do we let the bombarding of advertising, the constant flow of direct ('junk') mail encouraging us to buy further consumer inessentials, and the general inexorable pressures of the world squeeze us into the world's mould?

In short, what is the priority of our lives? How does it match up to Jesus' conclusion: 'Seek first his kingdom and his righteousness, and all these things will be given to you as well' (Matthew 6:33)?

- Work. Work is a gift of God (Genesis 2:15). It's his intention that we should enjoy it (Ecclesiastes 5:18–19). It's right to receive reasonable pay for work (Luke 3:14; 10:7). There are harsh words for those who refuse to work (2 Thessalonians 3:6–15).

- Sleep. 'He gives to his beloved sleep' (Psalm 127:2, RSV) is one of those verses I pray over in a half-waking manner after a hard day. We do need sleep. It is essential for our physical welfare. I recall one Christian leader saying how she would tell her students she was preparing for a meeting. This was her way of saying that she was sleeping! (I must add that her talks bore out her solid preparations as well!) Our lives need to be ordered so that we take good care of our bodies.

Our days

What does the Bible say about different human ages?
- Birth and growing up. What a privilege it is to see one's baby born – to see the contractions of labour yield a God-given new baby, 'fearfully and wonderfully made . . . in secret, and curiously wrought' (Psalm 139:14–15, Authorized (King James) Version). Children are a gift of God.

Do you know the promise given to children? 'Children, obey your parents in the Lord, for this is right. "Honour your father and mother" – which is the first commandment with a promise – "that it may go well with you and that you may enjoy long life on the earth" ' (Ephesians 6:1–3). The other part of the command is equally important: 'Fathers, do not exasperate your children; instead, bring them up in the training and instruction of the Lord' (Ephesians 6:4). What great responsibilities are placed upon parents to love and instruct their children; to teach them and train them (Deuteronomy 6:6–7; Proverbs 22:6; Matthew 19:13–15). Spurgeon has the following prayer on Genesis 17:7: 'O Lord, thou has made a covenant with me, thy servant, in Christ Jesus my Lord; and now, I beseech thee, let my children be included in its gracious provisions. Permit me to believe this promise as made to me as well as to Abraham. I know that my children are born in sin, and shapen in iniquity, even as those of other men; therefore, I ask nothing on the ground of their birth, for well I know that "that which is born of the flesh is flesh", and nothing more. Lord, make them to be born under thy covenant of grace by the Holy Spirit!'

• Marriage and home. Marriage is given by God (Genesis 2:18–25). Men and women joined in marriage are united by God (Matthew 19:4–6). A Christian may only marry a fellow believer (1 Corinthians 7:39). Marriage is therefore something serious, and should not be entered into lightly. It isn't 'more holy' to stay single, but it is far better to remain single and be happy than to marry and be unhappy. 'Heirs of the gracious gift of life' (1 Peter 3:7) is a description of a Christian husband and wife. What is the role of a husband to be? To love his wife (Ephesians 5:25, 28, 33; Colossians 3:19). Of a wife? To submit to her husband (Ephesians 5:22–33; Colossians 3:18).

What good Christian homes can be! The loving caring for children; the encouragement of other believers as we invite them to our homes. How difficult life at home can also be at times – when we are ourselves in all our weakness, where we have to learn the lessons of patience, selflessness and consideration in the 'rough and tumble' of home and family life.

● Middle life and old age. One minister I know said that no one was interested in the middle-aged. Youth groups, groups for young marrieds and Mums and Toddlers, Senior Citizen lunches, yes – but no one liked the middle-aged! Herbert Lockyer comments, 'The child of God knows that the "forty-ish" years are fine training for the future . . . to countless numbers of Christians, the joy in middle age is the unfailing friendship of God. Have you come to the meridian years of life? Then if you are the Lord's may He reawake your amazement at the marvels of His love, grant you the continuance of the child's unquestioning faith, enable you to retain your former modesty and meekness, and cause you to drink at the fountain of His undecaying strength.' An example: Caleb was sent to explore Canaan at 40 (Joshua 14:7).

And what about old age? The world believes that old age is something bad. Old people are 'has-beens', to be ignored or forgotten. The Bible says, however, that ageing believers aren't fading; old age can be a time of fruitfulness (Psalm 92:12–15). Some examples: Caleb wanted more challenges at 85 (Joshua 14:6–15). Anna, although old, still served God (Luke 2:36–38).

Whether our days are many or few, if we belong to God, we have the assurance that our strength will equal our days (Deuteronomy 33:25). God will prove himself to be our satisfying daily strength. Nothing is hidden from God; tomorrow is known to him and his promise is that strength will be sufficient for the needs and trials each day may bring. So let's not worry about tomorrow:

tomorrow can take care of itself; let's live one day at a time in the light of our faithful God.

Through all the changing scenes of life,
    In trouble and in joy,
The praises of my God shall still
    My heart and tongue employ.

Of His deliverance I will boast,
    Till all that are distressed
From my example comfort take,
    And charm their griefs to rest.

O magnify the Lord with me,
    With me exalt His Name;
When in distress to Him I called,
    He to my rescue came.

The hosts of God encamp around
    The dwellings of the just;
Deliverance He affords to all
    Who on His succour trust.

O make but trial of His love,
    Experience will decide
How blessed are they, and only they,
    Who in His truth confide.

Fear Him, ye saints, and you will then
    Have nothing else to fear;
Make you His service your delight,
    Your wants shall be His care.

Naham Tate, 1652–1715
and Nicholas Brady, 1659–1726

Conclusion

As we put God and his ways first in our lives, so Jesus promises that everything necessary for our well-being will be given to us.

'Seek first his kingdom and his righteousness, and all these things will be given to you as well' (Jesus, in Matthew 6:33).

8

WORKING IT OUT

Sent into the world

What are the priorities for us as Christians living in the world?

- *We are to be different from the world.* Look at the beginning of Jesus' 'Sermon on the Mount' (Matthew 5:3–12). Here he describes the type of people he wants his disciples to be. He calls us to have a radically different character from those around us: to know our own spiritual poverty, to be humble, to seek his righteousness first, to be compassionate, pure, peace-making. These beatitudes are in fact all promises! Do you want truly to have the earth's inheritance? Then be meek! Do you want a part in the kingdom of heaven? Then be poor in spirit! Do you want to see God . . .?

  The blessing in verse 10 has the same promise as the one in verse 3. And notice, too, that Jesus switches from 'they' to 'you' in verses 11 and 12, making it more personal.

  So as believers we are not to be 'of the world' (John 17:14, 16); our character is not derived from the world. Instead our character comes from God himself, because we belong to him.

- *We are to be involved in the world.* Move on in the Sermon on the Mount to Matthew 5:13–16. Jesus, sticking with the personal 'you', describes the role of believers in the world: we are to preserve what is good, what is of God, in today's society. We are to 'stop the rot'; we are to penetrate the world, have a positive influence on our surroundings.

In this sense we are sent into the world (John 17:15, 18); we have an impact on community life. So, how involved are we? Or are we so tied up in our church activities that there is no time or energy to be involved elsewhere?

This is the balance we must keep then. We must retain our saltiness and our brightness, our differentness from our environment, to be effective. And at the same time we must be in contact with the rotting, dark world. Then we will have the preserving, light-giving impact that God wants us to have and that the world is crying out for.

'As you sent me into the world, I have sent them into the world' (Jesus, in John 17:18).

Getting ready for the future

1

FACING DEATH

Key thought Death is the one certainty that faces us all.

Key Bible verse 'Man is destined to die once, and after that to face judgment' (Hebrews 9:27).

Death is the one thing that we all must face. We may have different backgrounds, occupations, and experiences of life, but we all have one thing in common: we all must die one day. Whatever age we live in, whatever our life is like, we must all come to the end of our days on this earth. Death is a certainty.

Death is an appointment

'Man is destined to die once' (Hebrews 9:27). Death itself is part of the punishment for human sin (Genesis 2:17; 3:19). Death is a universal, inevitable experience. And for each one of us the day that God has fixed for our death will surely come; there is 'a time to be born and a time to die' (Ecclesiastes 3:2). This speaks to us of God's good, acceptable, and perfect will. Hard though this is at times to understand, we may rest assured in God's timing. This doesn't remove our sense of loss, but it does remind us that, somehow, behind everything is the good purpose of almighty God.

Death is a departure

Jesus and the apostles Paul and Peter spoke of their deaths as a 'departure' (Luke 9:31; 2 Timothy 4:6; 2 Peter 1:15). We have to leave our present imperfect lives. Where are we going to? There is a separation of body and soul at death. The body decays (Genesis 3:19; Acts 13:36). The soul of believers passes into the glory of heaven (Psalm 73:24–25; Hebrews 12:23–24). There, believers experience full joy (Psalm 16:11), seeing God (Psalm 17:15; Revelation 22:4) and serving Christ (Revelation 7:15). Heaven is *home* (John 14:3), a place of eternal warmth, peace, and security. It is a place of being with others (Hebrews 12:22–23), where all is centred on the one 'who sits on the throne and . . . the Lamb' (Revelation 5:13). These things are true only because the curse of death due to us has been taken by Christ (Galatians 3:10–14). Unbelievers after death experience torment in hell, from which there is no escape (Luke 16:19–31).

Death is a benefit

For Christians, then, death is a benefit. Read again some of the comforting words used to describe the death of a Christian. The death of a Christian is:

- precious in the sight of the Lord (Psalm 116:15);
- a going to paradise (Luke 23:43);
- a going to our Father's house in which there are many rooms (John 14:2);
- a gain; being with Christ, which is better by far (Philippians 1:21, 23);
- at home with the Lord (2 Corinthians 5:8).

And so . . .?

What are we to do in the light of this teaching? Let's look
at two areas: coping with bereavement and facing up to
our own death.

- Coping with bereavement. 'Jesus wept' (John 11:35) is
  the shortest verse in the Bible. We see Jesus' deep
  emotions at the tomb of his friend. We, too, know sadness
  at the death of ones dear to us. Yet we can also be happy
  that if the person who has died is a believer then he or
  she is now with Christ (1 Thessalonians 4:13–14). Death
  does not separate us from God's love (Romans 8:38).
  There is also a responsibility for us to help those who
  have been bereaved (e.g. 1 Timothy 5:3–16; James 1:27).

- Facing up to death. Am I ready to die? Are you? Have
  we 'made our peace' with God? (By which the Bible
  means, have we been reconciled with God? Do we have
  a living personal relationship with him? Do we know
  that all our sin has been forgiven and we stand in a right
  relationship with our creator?) God urges you in an
  insistent yet tender way to turn to him *now* (John
  1:10–13; 3:15–18; 2 Corinthians 6:2).

  Have we been set free from the fear of death (Hebrews
  2:14–15)? Christ's resurrection means:
  □ Christ cannot die again; death no longer has mastery
  over him; he died to sin once for all (Romans 6:9–10).
  □ Christ is alive for ever and ever (Revelation 1:18).
  □ that forgiveness and justification are certainly ours
  now (Romans 4:25; 1 Corinthians 15:17).
  □ that we are raised with him to a new spiritual life
  (Romans 6:4–11; Ephesians 2:1–10; Colossians 3:1–11).

How are we to live prepared lives? Read Jim Packer's
practical advice: 'How may Christians live their lives
packed up and ready to go? There is no mystery about
it; common sense should tell us. Be wholly committed
to Christ's service each day. Don't touch sin with a

barge-pole. Keep short accounts with God. Think of each hour as God's gift to you, to make the most and best of. Plan your life, budgeting for seventy years (Psalm 90:10), and understanding that if your time proves shorter that will not be unfair deprivation but rapid promotion. Never let the good, or the not-so-good, crowd out the best, and cheerfully forgo what is not the best for the sake of what is. Live in the present; gratefully enjoy its pleasures and work through its pains with God, knowing that both the pleasures and the pains are steps on the journey home. Open all your life to the Lord Jesus and spend time consciously in his company, basking in and responding to his love. Say to yourself often that every day is one day nearer. Remember that, as George Whitefield said, man is immortal till his work is done (though God alone defines the work), and get on with what you know to be God's task for you here and now' (*God's Words*).

As Moses said, 'Teach us to number our days aright, that we may gain a heart of wisdom.' Luther suggested that this meant, 'Teach us so to think about death, that . . .' May we not be escapists, but face up to death realistically, being taken up with Christ, his kingdom and his ways here on earth. Then we will be ready to meet him in heaven.

> Lord, it belongs not to my care
>   Whether I die or live;
> To love and serve thee is my share,
>   And this thy grace must give.
>
> If life be long, I will be glad
>   That I may long obey;
> If short – yet why should I be sad
>   To soar to endless day?
>
> Christ leads me through no darker rooms
>   Than he went through before;

He that into God's kingdom comes
   Must enter by this door.

Then shall I end my sad complaints
   And weary sinful days,
And join with the triumphant saints
   That sing Jehovah's praise.

My knowledge of that life is small,
   The eye of faith is dim;
But it's enough that Christ knows all,
   And I shall be with him.

Richard Baxter, 1615–91

Conclusion
Are *you* ready to die?

'The time has come for my departure. I have fought the good fight, I have finished the race, I have kept the faith. Now there is in store for me the crown of righteousness, which the Lord, the righteous Judge, will award to me on that day – and not only to me, but also to all who have longed for his appearing' (Paul, in 2 Timothy 4:6–8).

2

THE PROMISE OF CHRIST'S SECOND COMING

> *Key thought* We are to look forward to the personal return of Christ at the end of the age.
>
> *Key Bible verse* 'But do not forget this one thing . . . With the Lord a day is like a thousand years, and a thousand years are like a day. The Lord is not slow in keeping his promise, as some understand slowness. He is patient with you, not wanting anyone to perish, but everyone to come to repentance. But the day of the Lord will come . . .' (2 Peter 3:8–10).

What is the world coming to?

Knowing God, trusting Jesus, growing in the Spirit, belonging to the church, living in the world – where is it all leading to? Where are we all going? Does the Bible say anything about our future? Yes! The answer is a resounding, glorious yes! The climax of the future is the second coming of Jesus.

There are over 250 references to Christ's return in the New Testament. Read through Matthew chapters 24 and 25, Mark 13, and Luke 21. Notice, too, these verses:

- 'And if I go and prepare a place for you, I will come back and take you to be with me that you also may be where I am' (John 14:3).
- 'This same Jesus, who has been taken from you into

heaven, will come back in the same way you have seen him go into heaven' (Acts 1:11).

- 'The Lord himself will come down from heaven, with a loud command, with the voice of the archangel and with the trumpet call of God' (1 Thessalonians 4:16).

- 'Christ was sacrificed once to take away the sins of many people; and he will appear a second time, not to bear sin, but to bring salvation to those who are waiting for him' (Hebrews 9:28).

- 'He who testifies to these things says, "Yes, I am coming soon" ' (Revelation 22:20).

What will the second coming be like?

'A full description of the Lord's return is impossible. In this event our glorified Lord will manifest himself in a manner which will be utterly climactic for existence as we know it. It will obviously therefore transcend all events in space and time hitherto experienced' (Bruce Milne). Bearing these comments in mind, what pointers does the Bible give us? The second coming will be:

- *glorious*. 'They will see the Son of Man coming on the clouds of the sky, with power and great glory' (Matthew 24:30). In contrast to the relative obscurity of Christ's first coming, the second coming will be personally clear to all: 'Every eye will see him' (Revelation 1:7). So Christ's second coming will be perceived by everyone.

- *sudden*. Christ will come at a time when we do not expect him (Matthew 24:44). His coming will be as unannounced as the arrival of a thief in the night (1 Thessalonians 5:2; 2 Peter 3:10).

When will Christ come again?

Christians have spent a lot of time and energy trying to work out an exact timetable for the events surrounding

Christ's second coming. In Mark 13 we're given an expressive picture of the irreligious state of the world before the end comes. New Testament chapters, for example 1 Timothy 4:1–3, 2 Timothy 3:1–9, and 2 Peter 3:3–7, describe similar tendencies. The figure of the antichrist is also associated with Christ's return (2 Thessalonians 2:1–12).

You see, much as some of us would like it, we're not given a precise, clearly marked schedule! The biblical emphasis is practical: *are we ready?* 'Keep watch, because you do not know on what day your Lord will come . . . so you . . . must be ready, because the Son of Man will come at an hour when you do not expect him' (Matthew 24:42, 44; see also Matthew 25:1–13). 'But do not forget this one thing . . . With the Lord a day is like a thousand years, and a thousand years are like a day. The Lord is not slow in keeping his promise, as some understand slowness. He is patient with you, not wanting anyone to perish, but everyone to come to repentance. But the day of the Lord will come . . .' (2 Peter 3:8–10).

Why will Christ come again?

- *To complete his work of salvation.* As Christians, we've already begun to experience salvation but there is much more in store for us (see 1 Thessalonians 4:17; 5:9; 1 John 3:2). God's kingdom – his rule – is already with us; but in the fullest sense, his kingdom will be established at Christ's coming (Luke 17:20–37). Christ's second coming will usher in a new creation. All the enemies of God – the devil, sin, and death – will be taken away (1 Corinthians 15:22–57; Revelation 12:7–11; 20:10). A new order will be established (2 Peter 3:10–13; Revelation 20, 21).

- *To bring about the resurrection.* Listen to Jesus' words, 'Do not be amazed at this, for a time is coming when all who

are in their graves will hear his voice and come out –
those who have done good will rise to live, and those
who have done evil will rise to be condemned' (John
5:28–29). Death is not the end; at Christ's coming all
who have ever lived will be restored to life . . . with a
view to judgment (see also 1 Corinthians 15:50–57;
1 Thessalonians 4:16–17).

● *To judge all people.* This is clearly taught in Scripture: in
the Old Testament, Psalm 110:6; Isaiah 61:2; Malachi
3:1–3; and in the New Testament, Matthew 16:27; John
5:21–23; Acts 17:31; 2 Corinthians 5:10; Hebrews 9:27;
Jude 14. All people will be judged. At the judgment
there will be a division between those who are acquitted
and those who are condemned to eternal punishment
(Daniel 12:2; Matthew 13:39–43; 25:31–46; John
5:28–29).

When the play is over . . .

I remember some years ago in York in the church where
David Watson ministered that a guest service was held
with the title 'When the play is over, the author walks on
to the stage'. The service was held, so far as I recall, during
the Mystery Play season – the series of dramas that describe
the biblical story from creation through to judgment. What
a powerful tool for evangelism at that time! And what a
message to a world that has lost its sense of direction! God
is saying: the world *is* going somewhere. More than this:
the end *will* come; history will come to a close. And: as the
final curtain falls at the end of time, the author *will* walk
on to the world's stage. Everyone *will* see him; Christ *will*
come!

> Lo! He comes with clouds descending,
>   Once for favoured sinners slain;
> Thousand thousand saints attending

Swell the triumph of His train:
  Hallelujah!
God appears on earth to reign.

Every eye shall now behold Him
  Robed in dreadful majesty;
Those who set at nought and sold Him,
  Pierced and nailed Him to the tree,
    Deeply wailing,
  Shall the true Messiah see.

Every island, sea, and mountain,
  Heaven and earth, shall flee away;
All who hate Him must, confounded,
  Hear the trump proclaim the day;
    Come to judgment!
  Come to judgment! come away!

Now redemption, long expected,
  See in solemn pomp appear!
All His saints, by man rejected,
  Now shall meet Him in the air:
    Hallelujah!
  See the day of God appear!

Yea, Amen! let all adore Thee,
  High on Thine eternal throne!
Saviour, take the power and glory;
  Claim the kingdom for Thine own:
    O come quickly!
  Hallelujah! come, Lord, come!

                    John Cennick, 1718–55
                and Charles Wesley, 1707–88

Conclusion

How are you preparing for Christ's second coming?

'I will come back and take you to be with me that you
also may be where I am' (Jesus, in John 14:3).

3

A FUTURE FULL OF PROMISES

Key thought The time is coming when all people who have ever lived will be judged by God.

Key Bible verse 'Do not be amazed at this, for a time is coming when all who are in their graves will hear his voice and come out – those who have done good will rise to live, and those who have done evil will rise to be condemned' (Jesus, in John 5:28–29).

The glorious resurrection

The resurrection of the dead is an important accompaniment to Christ's return. This event is touched on in the Old Testament (Job 19:25–27; Psalm 49:14–15; 73:24–26; Isaiah 26:19; Ezekiel 37:12; Daniel 12:2) and seen clearly in the New Testament (e.g. Matthew 22:29–32; John 5:25–29; 6:39–44; 1 Corinthians 15; Philippians 3:20–21; 1 John 3:1–3). It marks the completion of God's plan of redemption (Romans 8:23). It will be different from what we know at present. 'Flesh and blood cannot inherit the kingdom of God' (1 Corinthians 15:50); we will be given different, unperishable, and glorious bodies.

Then, death will have lost all its powers over believers (1 Corinthians 15:26). Even now, because of Christ's resurrection, death has lost its sting (1 Corinthians 15:55–56). And just as Christ has delivered our souls from the power of death (John 5:24; 1 John 3:14), so he *will* deliver our bodies (John 5:25–29).

God's righteous judgment

Everyone who has ever lived will have their lives judged by God. Nothing will be hidden; there will be an incomparable 'action replay' of our lives. What we really are, and what we have done and not done, will be brought to light. The basis of judgment will be the human response to God's revealed will. Different degrees of knowledge of God's will – and so differing abilities to fulfil this – will be taken into account (Matthew 11:21–24; Romans 2:12–16). God's judgment will be utterly righteous. All the injustices of the world will be put right and he will be shown to be perfectly just.

- Those who have rejected Christ will have this, their own choice, underlined (John 3:18–19; 2 Thessalonians 1:7–9).

- Those who have received Christ will be saved from condemnation. It is also taught in the Bible that the lives of Christians will be assessed for the quality of their work (1 Corinthians 3:10–15). But no true Christian will ever be lost.

The awfulness of hell

There will be a division at the last judgment between those who are acquitted and those who are condemned (Daniel 12:2; Matthew 13:39–43; John 5:28–29). Eternal punishment is taught in Scripture (Matthew 5:29; 10:28; 13:42, 50; 25:41; John 3:18–20, 36; Revelation 14:11). 'Those who remain unrepentant when confronted by God's claim on them, who reject his will when it is made known to them, and who continue through their lives in the blasphemy and rebellion which is implied, will face God's just wrath,' as Bruce Milne writes seriously in *Know the Truth*.

Satan will finally be 'tormented for ever and ever' (Revelation 21:10). The death of Christ on the cross has already meant that the devil is beaten (Colossians 2:15; 2 Timothy

1:10; Hebrews 2:14). He is still around, however, but the time is coming when the victory of the cross will be completed and Satan will be destroyed for ever.

A new heaven and a new earth

A new order is coming: the final consummation of everything (Isaiah 51:6; 65:17; 66:22; 2 Peter 3:13). All links with an old, sinful world will be completely destroyed. The gloriously renewed universe will know no sin or corruption, no more pain or illnesses. Read through Revelation 21:1–8 slowly to take it in!

Eternal issues

Thinking about these serious issues is important. I was on a crowded beach last summer; and the question flashed across my mind, 'Will God send these people to hell?' Do I really believe that those who reject Christ will suffer the eternal punishment of God's justice? I find it difficult to do so – and yet this is an inescapable part of the Bible message. How much more zealous this should make me in my praying for those who do not know the Saviour, and in my telling these same individuals the good news of Jesus!

And do I as a believer look forward to heaven? Do I contemplate what it will mean to enjoy Christ eternally? I wish I spent more time doing so now. I wish I would praise my Saviour more now, who bore that punishment due to me for my sin on the cross. It is only because of God's mercy and grace that I am saved from the punishment of hell.

Working it out

This teaching about the future is included in the Bible, not really to feed our curiosity, but to stir us up to be different people. In what ways?

- *Be hopeful.* Amidst the general pessimism of the world, Christians are to be hopeful: we know where the world is going; we know that God is Lord of his world. He will not – he cannot – lose his grip on the unfolding of his plan for the world.

- *Be comforted.* Because of Christ's resurrection, because of Christ's coming, we can be comforted, especially in times of bereavement, rather than 'grieve like the rest of men, who have no hope' (1 Thessalonians 4:13). And we are to 'encourage each other with these words' (1 Thessalonians 4:18).

- *Be holy.* Because our ultimate destination will be free of sin, 'since everything will be destroyed in this way, what kind of people ought you to be? You ought to live holy and godly lives as you look forward to the day of God and speed its coming' (2 Peter 3:11–12; see also 1 Thessalonians 5:23; 1 John 3:3).

- *Be active* – not idle (1 Thessalonians 5:14; 2 Thessalonians 3:6). We're to work faithfully, as good stewards (Luke 19:11–27) and patiently (James 5:7), giving ourselves fully to God's work (1 Corinthians 15:58):
  ☐ by spreading the gospel. It is after the gospel has been preached in the whole world, that 'then the end will come' (Matthew 24:14). May we be stirred on to complete the task of evangelizing the world!
  ☐by building up the church. When Christ returns, the church – all the people of God – will be presented to him as a bride to her husband (Revelation 21:2). Our task is to help make the church holy and pure, to be ready for her Lord.
  ☐by being involved in society. In the new universe, justice will reign and there will be true love and understanding. This shows us the sort of society that God wants now. Standing for social justice in our own age and world glorifies God.

- Be full of prayer. 'Your kingdom come' (Matthew 6:10) is part of the Lord's prayer; may we echo it.

- Be watchful, alert and ready – not completely wrapped up in the affairs of this world so that we neglect spiritual matters (Matthew 24:36–44). Our attitude can rightly be one of joyous anticipation of the fulfilling of God's great promises for the future.

> Thou Judge of quick and dead,
>   Before whose bar severe,
> With holy joy, or guilty dread,
>   We all shall soon appear;
> Our cautioned souls prepare
>   For that tremendous day,
> And fill us now with watchful care,
>   And stir us up to pray –
>
> To pray, and wait the hour,
>   That aweful hour unknown,
> When, robed in majesty and power,
>   Thou shalt from heaven come down,
> The immortal Son of Man,
>   To judge the human race,
> With all Thy Father's dazzling train,
>   With all Thy glorious grace.
>
> O may we thus be found
>   Obedient to His Word,
> Attentive to the trumpet's sound,
>   And looking for our Lord!
> O may we thus ensure
>   A lot among the blest;
> And watch a moment to secure
>   An everlasting rest!

Charles Wesley, 1707–88

Conclusion

God's plans for the future are meant to stir us into being different people for him now.

'Since everything will be destroyed in this way, what kind of people ought you to be? You ought to live holy and godly lives as you look forward to the day of God and speed its coming' (2 Peter 3:11–12).

4

THE SECURITY OF THE PROMISES

Key thought The security of God's promises rests in God himself.

Key Bible verse 'God has said, "Never will I leave you; never will I forsake you." So we say with confidence, "The Lord is my helper; I will not be afraid. What can man do to me?"' (Hebrews 13:5–6).

Spurgeon wrote once, 'I believe all the promises of God, but many of them I have personally tried and proved. I have seen that they are true, for they have been fulfilled to me.' In these closing pages, let us see how we can secure many of the promises of the Bible and make them our own.

We can distinguish between promises that have a condition attached to them, and those with no such condition. Promises with conditions are those that will be fulfilled when the requirements have been met. For example, 'Come to me, all you who are weary and burdened, and I will give you rest. Take my yoke upon you and learn from me, for I am gentle and humble in heart, and you will find rest for your souls' (Matthew 11:28–29). In order to find and enjoy Christ's rest, we must come to him, take his yoke upon us, and learn from him. A promise that has a condition attached to it can only become ours when the condition is recognized and acted on.

Other promises have no conditions attached to them.

God in his kindness towards his people says, 'Never will I leave you' (e.g. Hebrews 13:5). Such promises do not depend on what we deserve or on what we do; they are made out of God's free generosity. (Ultimately, all promises are like this: they depend solely on God's mercy and grace.)

To be practical . . .

Let's be specific. Suppose there is a particular area of your life that is causing you difficulty at the moment. It may be in your relationship with God or with others, at home, at work, at college. What steps can you take to let God's word come to you? Let me suggest the following:

● Find the promises.
● Let God speak to you.
● See if there are any conditions attached, and if so fulfil them.
● Continue to make the promise your own by praying it in and acting on it.

You may well be saying, *How* can I do these things? How can I find out God's promises? Well, this book has lots of them, for a start – but really the only way you're going to get to know the promises of the Bible is to read the Bible for yourself. Short guidelines on which verses to look up when you're feeling lonely, worried, etc., are helpful (e.g. p. 172), but even here there's a danger of taking verses out of context.

Let us suppose, however, you feel that God is far away. The verse 'Come near to God and he will come near to you' (James 4:8) springs to mind – perhaps via this book or some list of helps. You need to think about it, reflect on it, allow yourself to be deeply affected by it, take it in slowly. If there's a condition attached, then that needs to be acted on ('Come near to God', and see verse 7 and the end of verse 8). This means looking the verse up in your Bible; it also may mean looking at similar verses on a similar subject (a cross-reference Bible helps here) and thinking and praying about what it all means to you personally.

All this isn't meant to sound complicated: the simple idea is that God is speaking to you through his word! And he wants you to talk back to him (pray) about the promise. If it isn't working out in your experience, then don't hide that from him, but tell him so, honestly. Tell him about your *own* circumstances and difficulties. Maybe God requires some action of you, too – to say sorry to someone, to avoid watching certain types of films or videos. God wants *you* to be practical in working out the promises.

It can help to talk things over with a trusted friend – friends have a knack of putting their finger on things that we may well find difficult! It can also help to write down promises that mean a lot to you. You could write them on cards, pinning them on to a board, or in a note-book (perhaps with other thoughts and prayers).

The security of the promises

God's promises aren't magic formulae that you can read like a horoscope. They're part of his word, his message to us. That's why it's important to get to know the overall message of the Bible. As you do this, you'll get to know the God of the promises – the one who is utterly dependable.

- God's promises are true because God is *faithful*. 'He who promised is faithful' (Hebrews 10:23). God does not lie (Titus 1:2); he is dependable (Hebrews 6:16–20).

- God's promises are true because God is *powerful*. He has power to do what he promises (Romans 4:21). We can depend on God's promises because his power will never fail us.

> Jesus, my strength, my hope,
>   On Thee I cast my care,

With humble confidence look up,
   And know Thou hear'st my prayer.
Give me on Thee to wait,
   Till I can all things do,
On Thee, almighty to create,
   Almighty to renew.

I want a godly fear,
   A quick-discerning eye
That looks to Thee when sin is near,
   And sees the tempter fly;
A spirit still prepared,
   And armed with jealous care,
For ever standing on its guard
   And watching unto prayer.

I want a true regard,
   A single, steady aim,
Unmoved by threatening or reward,
   To Thee and Thy great Name;
A jealous, just concern
   For Thine immortal praise;
A pure desire that all may learn
   And glorify Thy grace.

I rest upon Thy Word;
   The promise is for me;
My succour and salvation, Lord,
   Shall surely come from Thee:
But let me still abide,
   Nor from my hope remove,
Till Thou my patient spirit guide
   Into Thy perfect love.

                  Charles Wesley, 1707–88

Conclusion

It takes time to learn to be dependent on God; but while we are learning – and we never really stop learning – he will never let us down.

'He who promised is faithful' (Hebrews 10:23).

5

MAKING THE PROMISES OUR OWN

> *Key thought* God's promises are given, not just to be read, but to be realized; not to be floating around, but to be fulfilled in and through us.
>
> *Key Bible verse* 'He [Abraham] did not waver through unbelief regarding the promise of God, but was strengthened in his faith and gave glory to God, being fully persuaded that God had power to do what he had promised' (Romans 4:20–21).

Promises are to be received by faith

The Christian life is a life of patient faith in God and his promises. Read through the following:

- 'What was promised, being given through faith in Jesus Christ, might be given to those who believe' (Galatians 3:22).

- 'We do not want you to become lazy, but to imitate those who through faith and patience inherit what has been promised' (Hebrews 6:12).

- 'And so after waiting patiently, Abraham received what was promised' (Hebrews 6:15).

- '. . . who through faith . . . gained what was promised' (Hebrews 11:33).

Some of God's promises may stagger us. They appear too

good to be true. But God means all that he says. Our difficulty sometimes is our failure to meet God's great promises with faith. We think we have to muster up great faith, but we find this a real problem. Surely it's more a matter of some faith, however small (Matthew 17:20), in our great God. Faith is a matter of looking to God, not to ourselves. 'You strengthen your faith . . . by looking hard at its objects – the promises of God in Scripture; the unseen realities of God and your life with him and your hope of glory; the living Christ himself, once on the cross, now on the throne' (J. I. Packer, *God's Words*).

In trying to muster up our own faith, we make the mistake of thinking of faith as a work. In other words, we may think we can earn a promise from God because of our faith. No! Faith is *how we receive God's promises*; it's the vehicle by which they come to us.

Promises are to be worked out in obedience

Herbert Lockyer rightly notes 'faith and obedience are the two legs a Christian walks with'. (Remember the hymn with the chorus, 'Trust and obey! For there's no other way to be happy in Jesus – But to trust and obey'?)

- 'All these blessings will come upon you and accompany you if you obey the LORD your God' (Deuteronomy 28:2).

- 'Those who honour me I will honour' (1 Samuel 2:30).

- 'To obey is better than sacrifice' (1 Samuel 15:22).

- 'If you are willing and obedient, you will eat the best from the land' (Isaiah 1:19).

- 'If only you had paid attention to my commands, your peace would have been like a river' (Isaiah 48:18).

- 'Obey me, and I will be your God and you will be my people' (Jeremiah 7:23).

- 'Not everyone who says to me, "Lord, Lord" will enter

the kingdom of heaven, but only he who does the will of my Father who is in heaven' (Matthew 7:21).

● 'Now that you know these things, you will be blessed if you do them' (John 13:17).

● 'Whoever has my commands and obeys them, he is the one who loves me' (John 14:21).

● 'You need to persevere so that when you have done the will of God, you will receive what he has promised' (Hebrews 10:36).

● 'Do not merely listen to the word, and so deceive yourselves. Do what it says' (James 1:22).

● 'We know that we have come to know him if we obey his commands' (1 John 2:3).

Obedience and disobedience are given as points of contrast between the saved and the lost. True Christians are 'obedient children' (1 Peter 1:14); those dead in their sins are 'disobedient' (Ephesians 2:2). Yet thank God there is a way to move from being disobedient to obedient: 'Thanks be to God that, though you used to be slaves to sin, you wholeheartedly obeyed the form of teaching to which you were entrusted. You have been set free from sin and have become slaves to righteousness' (Romans 6:17–18).

Are there areas in your life, in my life, in which we are holding out against God? Is he telling us to do something – or not to do something – and are we ignoring him? In claiming promises, we must honestly face any conditions attached to them. Then, with God's grace and help, we need to act on God's word. If we don't obey God, then we won't obtain his promises. Obedience is absolutely crucial.

Promises are to be presented in prayer

Read David's prayer: 'O Sovereign LORD, you are God! Your words are trustworthy, and you have promised these good things to your servant. Now be pleased to bless the house of your servant . . .' (2 Samuel 7:28–29).

In Psalm 119 the phrases 'according to your word' and 'according to your promise' occur several times (verses 25, 28, 41, 58, 76, 107, 116, 154, 169, 170). For an example of this, look up Daniel chapter 9. Daniel knew God's word and because he did so, he prayed (verses 2 and 3). Read Stuart Olyott's helpful comments from *Dare to Stand Alone*: 'Daniel did not say to himself, "God has promised that it will happen, therefore whatever I do, or do not do, it will happen." His logic is entirely different. It went like this: "God has said that after seventy years we can go home. That is the divine promise. Therefore I will pray to Him to turn away His anger from Jerusalem, and to bring the promised return to pass."

'Too often in history people have made God's promises an excuse for doing nothing. Their approach has been fatalistic and they have sat in idleness, waiting for the promise to be fulfilled. Daniel knew nothing of such an approach. To him the divine promise was a *reason* to engage in the hard work of prayer, not an excuse for inactivity. He resolved to beseech his God to be favourable once more to Jerusalem. Within a few months Darius was gone, and Cyrus stood up to announce that the Jews could go home!

'God had promised it. Daniel prayed for it. And it happened!

'Whatever other lessons we learn from this chapter, we must be sure to grasp this one. The cause of God's acting in history is not simply His promise, but also the prayer of His people. This is what praying "according to His will" is all about. This is a subject on which the New Testament often speaks, and it is a frighteningly simple concept. Praying according to the will of God is finding out from the Scriptures what God has promised and praying for that.'

God's unfailing promises are given to stimulate our prayers, to be used as the basis for our prayers. We can confidently ask for whatever is included in them. As Herbert

Lockyer puts it, 'The "fire" of our prayers must be fed with the "fuel" of divine promises.'

Spurgeon wrote a book of precious Bible promises for daily use, entitled *Faith's Checkbook* (cheque-book). In its preface, he wrote: 'A promise from God may very instructively be compared to a check payable to order. It is given to the believer with the view of bestowing upon him some good thing. It is not meant that he should read it over comfortably, and then have done with it. No, he is to treat the promise as a reality, as a man treats a check.

'He is to take the promise, and endorse it with his own name by personally receiving it as true. He is by faith to *accept* it as his own. He sets to his seal that God is true, and true as to this particular word of promise. He goes further, and believes that he has the blessing in having the sure promise of it, and therefore he puts his name to it to testify to the receipt of the blessing.

'This done, he must believingly *present* the promise to the Lord, as a man presents a check at the counter of the bank. He must plead it by prayer, expecting to have it fulfilled. If he has come to Heaven's bank at the right date, he will receive the promised amount at once. If the date should happen to be further on, he must patiently wait till its arrival; but meanwhile he may count the promise as money, for the bank is sure to pay when the due time arrives.

'Some fail to place the endorsement of faith upon the check, and so they get nothing; and others are slack in presenting it, and these also receive nothing. This is not the fault of the promise, but of those who do not act with it in a common-sense, business-like manner. God has given no pledge which He will not redeem, and encouraged no hope which He will not fulfil.'

> I'm not ashamed to own my Lord,
>   Or to defend His cause;

Maintain the honour of His Word,
    The glory of His cross.

Jesus, my God! I know His Name,
    His Name is all my trust;
Nor will He put my soul to shame,
    Nor let my hope be lost.

Firm as His throne His promise stands,
    And He can well secure
What I've committed to His hands
    Till the decisive hour.

Then will He own my worthless name
    Before His Father's face;
And, in the new Jerusalem,
    Appoint my soul a place.

                    Isaac Watts, 1674–1748

Conclusion

How are you doing? God's promises are secure. The way to make his promises our own is to live our life with God. As we trust him, doing what he wants and presenting his promises in prayer, we can be confident that his promises will be fulfilled.

'By faith Abraham . . . obeyed and went, even though he did not know where he was going' (Hebrews 11:8).

6

THE SUBSTANCE OF THE PROMISES

> *Key thought* The promises of God are fulfilled for us in Christ.
>
> *Key Bible verse* 'The promise of life that is in Christ Jesus' (2 Timothy 1:1).

The riches of the promises

How many promises are there in the Bible? Estimates range from around 8000 to 30,000 (about the number of verses in the whole Bible). Whatever the precise figure is, what is certain is that there is a great wealth in the Bible's precious promises.

Promises, promises

We all get tired of people around us making promises that they don't keep. Before elections politicians woo voters with promises that turn to empty words a few months or years later. A man may promise 'to have and to hold [his wife] from this day forward, for better for worse . . .' in the marriage ceremony only for this promise to turn sour later. The writer Thomas Fuller said, 'A man apt to promise is apt to forget', and Jonathan Swift, 'Promises and pie-crust are made to be broken'; a proverb runs 'He that promises too much means nothing.' We're all too familiar with broken promises.

With God, however, things are different. As we have seen several times in this book, we can depend utterly on God and the promises he makes. His promises are not mere mental decisions to give a benefit; they are firm declarations of intent that he is bound to fulfil.

The crown of the promises

'No matter how many promises God has made, they are "Yes" in Christ' (2 Corinthians 1:20). God's promises come to us through Christ. They're summed up in the person of our Saviour, the Lord Jesus Christ. As Herbert Lockyer puts it, 'All these promises are "of God, in him", that is the Saviour. The Father committed to the Son the bounties of His grace to give to men, and they can only receive them as they come to Him. All from God is in Christ Jesus.' Or read David Prior's words from *The Suffering and the Glory*: 'In Jesus God has said, and continues to say, "Yes" to us. Everything he has ever promised us he has made good in Jesus. Has God offered to forgive our sins? We have forgiveness in Jesus. Has God promised never to fail us or forsake us? We have the presence of God with us in Jesus to the end of time. Has God promised to put a new heart and a new spirit within us? Through Jesus we have the gift of the Holy Spirit. Has God promised to call us his own sons and daughters, to guide us and provide for us? We are children of God in his Son, Jesus, and this God will be our guide for ever. Has God promised us eternal life and an inheritance in heaven? These gifts are ours in Jesus. "God has never put a hope or a prayer into man's heart that is not answered and satisfied abundantly in his Son" (James Denney). In every way, therefore, God has demonstrated his positive commitment to us in Jesus.'

This verse from 2 Corinthians also means that all the Old Testament promises of God are fulfilled in Jesus Christ. We saw in an earlier section (p. 33) the incredible number of prophecies about Jesus that have been fulfilled at his first coming. We also see fulfilled in him the Old Testament law and the prophets (Matthew 5:17). We have seen the fulfilment of the promise of the coming of the Holy Spirit (p. 71). And we await the fulfilment of prophecies concerning Christ's second coming (p. 204).

What is our response to all this? God's 'Yes' in Christ is echoed by our saying 'Yes indeed' (Amen) in worship, to the glory of God (end of 2 Corinthians 1:20).

What is the guarantee of God keeping his promises? Look at 2 Corinthians 1:21–22: 'All the unchangeable character of God the Holy Trinity lies behind this grace in salvation', as David Prior puts it. God makes us 'stand firm in Christ. He anointed us, set his seal of ownership on us, and put his Spirit in our hearts as a deposit, guaranteeing what is to come.' What utter commitment by God to us! What reliability!

Where is it all leading to?

Read 2 Peter 1:3–4: 'His divine power has given us everything we need for life and godliness through our knowledge of him who called us by his own glory and goodness. Through these he has given us his very great and precious promises, so that through them you may participate in the divine nature and escape the corruption in the world caused by evil desires.'

The Lord's promises come to us through his glory and goodness. What is the result of his promises, his power, his person? Expressed in the most supremely positive way: we share in what God is like (we 'participate in the divine nature') as we (here's the negative) turn our backs on, or flee from, this rebellious world's degeneracy. So the promises provide an incentive and encouragement to a life of holiness (see also 2 Corinthians 7:1). 'At all times, our eyes must be fixed, not on a promise merely, but on Him, the only Foundation of our hopes, and in and through whom alone all the promises are made good to us: also upon the

Holy Spirit the Comforter, through whose grace we discover the excellency and blessedness of the promises' (Herbert Lockyer).

> Jesus, I am resting, resting
>   In the joy of what Thou art;
> I am finding out the greatness
>   Of Thy loving heart.
> Thou hast bid me gaze upon Thee,
>   And Thy beauty fills my soul,
> For by Thy transforming power
>   Thou hast made me whole.

> *Jesus, I am resting, resting*
>   *In the joy of what Thou art;*
> *I am finding out the greatness*
>   *Of Thy loving heart.*

> O how great Thy lovingkindness,
>   Vaster, broader than the sea!
> O how marvellous Thy goodness,
>   Lavished all on me!
> Yes, I rest in Thee, Belovèd,
>   Know what wealth of grace is Thine,
> Know Thy certainty of promise,
>   And have made it mine.

> Simply trusting Thee, Lord Jesus,
>   I behold Thee as Thou art,
> And Thy love, so pure, so changeless,
>   Satisfies my heart;
> Satisfies its deepest longings,
>   Meets, supplies its every need,
> Compasseth me round with blessings,
>   Thine is love indeed!

> Ever lift Thy face upon me,
>   As I work and wait for Thee;
> Resting 'neath Thy smile, Lord Jesus,

Earth's dark shadows flee.
Brightness of my Father's glory,
    Sunshine of my Father's face,
Keep me ever trusting, resting;
    Fill me with Thy grace.

Jean Sophia Pigott, 1845–82

Conclusion
As we consider God's promises and trust in Jesus, we
come to know God more and lead lives that honour
him.

'No matter how many promises God has made, they
are "Yes" in Christ' (2 Corinthians 1:20).

7

LIVING IN THE LIGHT OF THE PROMISES

Key thought We can learn from the examples of two New Testament believers what it means to live in the light of God's promises.

Key Bible verse 'We . . . want you . . . to imitate those who through faith and patience inherit what has been promised' (Hebrews 6:12).

What characteristics mark out the life of a Christian who is living in the light of the promises of God? Let's look at two of the people who feature in the story about the events after the birth of Christ and see what we can learn from them: Simeon and Anna. You recall, Joseph and Mary were bringing their first baby boy to present him in the temple.

Simeon: Luke 2:25–35

Simeon was:
● righteous and devout (verse 25). This combination 'may well indicate that Simeon conducted himself in such a manner that his behavior both with respect to men . . . and God . . . was the object of God's approval' (William Hendriksen). Are you living a good life – with God, and with those around you? Do you have a 'couldn't-care-less' attitude to the things of God? Are you solely content

to look after 'number one' – yourself? Or are you eager and careful to do what God has given you to do?

● 'waiting for the consolation of Israel' (verse 25). Others were, too (verse 38). They were aware of the dark times they lived in, politically, socially, and religiously. But they took prophecy seriously: they were expectant for God to act; they were patiently waiting for the Messiah's coming. And us? Do we ignore the prophecies and promises of God – or do we have the certain hope of him coming to us? Read again the promises and prophecies of Christ's second coming (p. 204). Christ is certainly coming again! What a glorious hope!

● influenced by the Holy Spirit: the 'Holy Spirit was upon him' (verse 26). The Spirit had shown him that he would not die before he had seen the Lord's Christ. The Spirit guided him into the temple (verse 27). He met up with Jesus' parents, took the child Jesus in his arms and blessed God (verse 28). He thanked God, the sovereign Lord, for what the child meant to him personally and to the wide world – both Gentiles (for whom salvation is light) and Jews (for whom salvation is glory). He thanked God that he had lived long enough to see the Messiah. Now he was ready to die (verses 29–32).

Simeon then blessed the parents, adding amazing words to Mary. Her child would, according to God's plan, divide people and point people to God. Their reaction to him would show their real spiritual condition. Mary, herself, would suffer intense anguish (verses 33–35).

What can we learn from this? To seek constantly the presence of the Holy Spirit; to know that God is always sovereign; to ensure that our hearts are right with God.

Anna: Luke 2:36–38

Anna was:

- a widow, very old – at least 84 – yet still active! She was a prophetess – she declared to others the revelations God gave her. I like the phrase 'she never left the temple' (verse 37). It reminds me of some faithful older believers who joyfully attend the church services on a Sunday and all the meetings through the week – they virtually live at the church!

- a constant worshipper of God, with her fasting and praying (verse 37). How about the fasting? Remember Jesus' words 'When you fast . . .' (Matthew 6:16), which seem to imply we will: he doesn't say 'If you fast . . .'! Of course fasting *in the right spirit* is vital (Matthew 6:16–17); but surely we're missing out on part of what God wants us to do if we neglect fasting altogether (see also 2 Samuel 1:11–12; Isaiah 58:6–12; Acts 13:2–3).

  Anna was *serious* in her worship: she was concerned for God's kingdom. Anna then joined the little group: Jesus, Joseph, Mary, and Simeon. Her thankfulness overspilled in prayer to God, and then to all the others who were about her waiting for the salvation of Jerusalem (verse 38). What an example Anna is to young and old: a life of worship, fasting, prayer, thankfulness, telling others about the Christ! How do we match up to her devotion, faithfulness, and zeal?

And us?

So there it is: two seemingly insignificant people from God's word who were humble yet confident, faithful yet expectant, worshippers of God yet also concerned for their fellow human beings. Is it all too good to be true? These people seem, in a way, so perfect. And yet they weren't: Simeon needed the salvation he was waiting for (verse 30); he was an ordinary 'man in Jerusalem' (verse 25); he remained God's servant (verse 29).

And Anna: well, her name means 'grace', her background was the family Phanuel (the place-name *Peniel*, which means 'face of God', named such by Jacob because he had seen God face to face, yet his life was spared, Genesis 32:30). She was of the tribe of Asher, Jacob's eighth son, way back in Israel's history! So her family had certainly 'seen life' and must surely have known its ups and downs.

Why do I say this? Because Simeon and Anna weren't 'wax-work' believers. They were flesh and blood. They weren't perfect. And neither are we. Yet in their faith, in their struggles, they remained devoted to God. They lived their lives in the light of the promises of God. They served him loyally through their lives. And we're to follow their (and countless others') examples.

> The Lord is King; lift up thy voice,
> O earth, and all ye heavens rejoice!
> From world to world the joy shall ring:
> 'The Lord Omnipotent is King!'
>
> The Lord is King! who then shall dare
> Resist His will, distrust His care,
> Or murmur at His wise decrees,
> Or doubt His royal promises?
>
> The Lord is King! child of the dust,
> The Judge of all the earth is just:
> Holy and true are all His ways;
> Let every creature speak His praise.
>
> He reigns! ye saints, exalt your strains:
> Your God is King, your Father reigns;
> And He is at the Father's side,
> The Man of love, the Crucified.
>
> Come, make your wants, your burdens known:

He will present them at the throne;
And angel bands are waiting there,
His messages of love to bear.

One Lord, one empire, all secures:
He reigns – and life and death are yours;
Through earth and heaven one song shall ring,
'The Lord Omnipotent is King!'

Josiah Conder, 1789–1855

Conclusion
Our lives – our joys, our struggles, our failures, our sins – will in some ways be similar to those of Simeon and Anna; in other ways, different. And yet we may all trust in the same God, the giver of our salvation in Christ.

'My eyes have seen your salvation, which you have prepared in the sight of all people, a light for revelation to the Gentiles and for glory to your people Israel' (Luke 2:30–32).

8

WORKING IT OUT

His precious promises

Let's review where our thinking about God's promises has brought us to.

The God of the promises

'His very great and precious promises' (2 Peter 1:4) come from God our Father, through the Lord Jesus Christ, by the Holy Spirit.

We have seen that God is faithful and dependable: so different from us, yet also so near to us in Christ.

We have seen that God is the author of the promises and he wants the promises to become real for us. They become real for us, as we believe on him, making him and his promise of life our own (John 1:12; 2 Timothy 1:1). They become real as we immerse ourselves in his word, the Bible, by staying close to him, by opening up our lives to Jesus and his Spirit.

Promises for now

All of us struggle; none of us has 'got it all together'. So we need to take God's promises to heart in the here and now of our lives, in the world's rough and tumble. Christian truth isn't meant just to be true for special Christian holidays or conferences: it has to be worked out and worked at in the nitty-gritty of ordinary living.

We need others' help in this. That's why God wants us to be part of a local church, where we can give of ourselves to others and receive from them. We are 'sharers together in the promise in Christ Jesus' (Ephesians 3:6).

As we have seen, God's purposes for us are that we should be like him – holy, different from those around us. We're to show the fruit of his Holy Spirit in our lives (see Galatians 5:22–23) as we live for him in the world. How are you doing?

But God's promises don't only present a challenge to us. Perhaps more predominantly they present an encouragement to us – of his constant never-failing love (read Romans 8:28–39).

Promises for the future

God's promises aren't only for present times. They're for our own personal futures, whatever they hold; but most gloriously what is utterly inconceivable to our present thinking – that we will be with Christ for ever and ever: 'We know that when he appears, we shall be like him, for we shall see him as he is' (1 John 3:2). We will be with Jesus and will see his glory (John 17:24). We will receive the crown of righteousness, life, and glory (2 Timothy 4:8; James 1:12; 1 Peter 5:4). What a glorious future! Yet something of this is even now going on at the moment: 'We, who with unveiled faces all reflect the Lord's glory, are being transformed into his likeness with ever-increasing glory, which comes from the Lord, who is the Spirit' (2 Corinthians 3:18). What a great and precious promise!

'His divine power has given us everything we need for life and godliness through our knowledge of him who called us by his own glory and goodness. Through these he has given us his very great and precious promises, so that through them you may participate in the divine nature and escape the corruption in the world caused by evil desires' (2 Peter 1:3–4).

BIBLIOGRAPHY

Ann Alexander, Fay Blix, *The Student Promise Pocketbook* (Harold Shaw).

Horatius Bonar, *The Word of Promise* (Religious Tract Society).

F. F. Bruce (ed.), *Promise and Fulfilment* (T. & T. Clark).

Samuel Clarke, *A Collection of the Promises of Scripture* (Chas. J. Thynne).

Michael Green, *Evangelism – now and then* (Inter-Varsity Press).

Michael Griffiths, *Cinderella with amnesia* (Inter-Varsity Press).

Herbert Lockyer, *All the Promises of the Bible* (Zondervan).

Bruce Milne, *Know the Truth* (Inter-Varsity Press).

G. Campbell Morgan, *The Spirit of God* (Hodder & Stoughton).

J. I. Packer, *God's Words* (Inter-Varsity Press).

J. I. Packer, *Keep in Step With the Spirit* (Inter-Varsity Press).

J. I. Packer, *Knowing God* (Hodder & Stoughton).

Charles H. Spurgeon, *Faith's Checkbook* (Moody Press).

David Watson, *I believe in the Church* (Hodder & Stoughton).

David Watson, *One in the Spirit* (Hodder & Stoughton).

John White, *The Fight* (Inter-Varsity Press).

SUBJECT INDEX

Saints, 117
Salvation, 38, 145
Sanctification, 86

Satan, 141
Second coming of Jesus, 204
Self-control, 94
Sin, 39
– forgiveness of, 54
– God's promises to us concerning, 172
Sleep, God's provision of, 192
Spirit *see* Holy Spirit
Spiritual warfare, 142
Strength, promise of, 166
Sword of the Spirit, 145

Teaching, 131
Tired, promises when, 173
Tithing, 127, 191
Truth, 82, 143

Union with Christ, 87
Unity, of the church, 147

Warfare, spiritual, 142
Weak, promises when, 173
Word of God, 155
Work, 192
World, life in the, 155
Worried, promises when, 172
Worship, 129

BIBLICAL INDEX